Couns

Also by Kathryn Geldard and David Geldard:

Working with Children in Groups: A Handbook for Counsellors, Educators and Community Workers *

Counselling Adolescents: The Proactive Approach

Counselling Children: A Practical Introduction

Basic Personal Counselling: A Training Manual for Counsellors (4th edn)

* also published by Palgrave Macmillan

Counselling Skills in Everyday Life

KATHRYN GELDARD

and

DAVID GELDARD

First published 2003 by
PALGRAVE MACMILLAN
Houndmills, Basingstoke, Hampshire RG21 6XS and
175 Fifth Avenue, New York, N.Y. 10010
Companies and representatives throughout the world

PALGRAVE MACMILLAN is the global academic imprint of the Palgrave Macmillan division of St. Martin's Press, LLC and of Palgrave Macmillan Ltd. Macmillan® is a registered trademark in the United States, United Kingdom and other countries. Palgrave is a registered trademark in the European Union and other countries.

ISBN 1–4039–0313–1 paperback

This book is printed on paper suitable for recycling and made from fully managed and sustained forest sources.

A catalogue record for this book is available from the British Library.

Editing and origination by Aardvark Editorial, Mendham, Suffolk

*This book is dedicated to Lavinia Leslie
who has demonstrated special expertise in
using counselling skills in her everyday life*

Contents

1 What are counselling skills?

The first thing we did as we sat down in front of our computers to write this book was to think about life as it is today. For a while, instead of writing, we chatted about common values that seem to be fashionable and respected. We thought about the way that today many people place a high value on independence and self-sufficiency. We ourselves are people who value our independence and pride ourselves on being self-sufficient. We work for ourselves in our own counselling practice and as writers and trainers. Even so, we recognise that at times we need to seek each other's or someone else's help. We think that it is sensible for us to value our boundaries and to generally be independent, but to be flexible enough to look for and/or accept help when we need it.

How do you see yourself? Do you see yourself primarily as someone who is independent and self-sufficient? If so, are you someone who lives a fairly solitary life, or someone who is actively part of an extended family, social system, or wider community? We are all different; some of us choose to be very independent and self-sufficient whereas others value a more cooperative lifestyle.

Because there is currently a strong emphasis on self-sufficiency some people believe that everyone should look after their own needs without help from others. If we accept this point of view we won't seek help ourselves, or give help to other people. Sadly, such an attitude is likely to result in an uncaring society where everyone puts self-interest above the needs of others. We do need to recognise though that such an attitude is understandable. Some people live such pressured lives that they do not have the energy to care for others while at the same time looking after their own needs. Fortunately, in spite of the fast pace of modern life, there are many people who are prepared, and able, to give something of themselves in order to help others.

One of the most useful ways in which we can help other people is to listen and communicate with them in ways that enable them to share their troubles and feel better. In this book we will describe a number of listening, communication and helping skills. These skills are basic counselling skills that are used, along with other skills and strategies, by volunteer and professional counsellors when counselling people who have specifically sought counselling help.

The counselling skills that we will discuss in this book are extremely useful ones because they are generally applicable, not just in a counselling situation, but in a wide range of life situations. It is therefore exciting for us to write this book and to be able to share with you our ideas about how to use these skills in everyday life. As we write, we both remember what it was like for us when we first learnt to make use of counselling skills. At that time we had many questions about whether it was appropriate for us to be learning to help other people in this way. Because we are human, we had our own problems and therefore found ourselves asking the question, 'What kind of people use counselling skills; are they limited to use by counsellors or can some of these skills be used in everyday life?'

> One of the most useful ways of helping other people is to be effective in listening and communicating with them

WHO CAN USE COUNSELLING SKILLS?

Because you are reading this book, we assume that you would like to learn some counselling skills that are suitable for use in everyday life. As we sit here writing we find ourselves wondering who you, the reader, are. Are you a person who works at home looking after yourself or your family; are you someone who is a member of a religious organisation; do you work in an office or a factory; are you a tradesman or a professional, a medical practitioner, a nursing sister, a child care worker, an accountant,

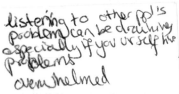

listening to other ppl's
problems can be draining
especially if you ur self have
problems — overwhelmed

you are the president of your social club, or sports club, or run a youth group. Alternatively, you may be a quiet, retiring person who fades into the background socially and never takes a leadership role.

You might want to take a moment to think about who you are, and to think about three things that you like about yourself.

Three things I like about myself are:

1. ....

2. ....

3. ....

We suggested that you write down three things you like about yourself because if you like yourself you probably feel good about who you are. If you feel good about yourself you are in a position to help other people feel good about themselves. We would like to make it clear that it doesn't matter who you are, what your lifestyle is, or what you do for a living. The counselling skills we will describe can be used by people from all walks of life and in a wide variety of situations.

Do you have personal problems of your own? It is quite possible that you do. We have come to the conclusion that there are very few people, if any, who do not have problems of some sort. Don't despair; having problems does not preclude you from helping others. However, we would like to give you a word of caution. If you decide to make use of counselling skills it is likely that other people will share some of their problems and troubling thoughts with you. Listening to other people's problems can be emotionally draining. This will be particularly so if you yourself have problems that continually intrude into your life. If you do, your problems may seriously interfere with your ability to be effective in helping others. Additionally, you might become overwhelmed by being burdened with other people's problems as well as your own. Clearly, the impact on you if you use counselling skills is an important consideration so we will explore this more fully later. Of course there may also be benefits for you if you learn to use counselling skills effectively as not only will you have the satisfaction of helping other people, but also your relationships may improve.

Helping others deal with day-to-day problems isn't an activity that is restricted to highly qualified professionals. On the contrary, it's an activity that most people do from time to time when the need arises. It is an activity which occurs naturally and which we all learn from childhood onwards. I am sure that you can remember a time when you listened to someone who was distressed and helped them feel better.

We hope that by reading this book you will be able to develop skills which will enhance your current ability to listen and help others, either in a social setting or in a work environment. We think that this book should be particularly useful to anyone who works directly with people, regardless of the nature or context of their work. For example, we believe that it will be helpful for those who work within health and social care settings, advice and welfare agencies, youth programmes, the legal services, housing services, charitable and voluntary organisations, emergency services, and for religious or spiritual leaders, teachers, informal carers, and other interested people.

Have you noticed that some people have a natural talent for listening to other people and helping them to sort out their problems? If you have a natural talent you will probably find that people seem to seek you out when they have something on their mind that is bothering them. Quite clearly, we all have different levels of competence and success in our ability to join with and listen to other people, but we believe that by learning some specific skills we can be more effective in helping others.

Do you think that you have a high level of naturally acquired counselling skills? You may have. Whether you have or not, our hope is that by reading this book you will be able to discover ways to be more effective when using counselling skills and will also gain a better understanding of the processes which occur when these skills are used.

IF I USE COUNSELLING SKILLS WILL I BE A COUNSELLOR?

The short answer to this question is 'No'. It is important to be clear about the difference between making use of some basic counselling skills in everyday life and counselling. They are not the same, although they lie on the same continuum (see Chapter 10). So that you can understand the difference between counselling and using counselling skills in everyday life we will discuss:

- Counselling
- The use of counselling skills.

> Counselling is significantly different from using counselling skills in everyday life

Counselling

Although this book is intended to help readers learn some basic counselling skills for use in everyday life it is not intended to help readers become counsellors. Even so, we realise that it is possible that some readers may become so enthused by the success that they have in using the skills we describe that they may decide to undertake training to become counsellors.

Anyone wanting to become a counsellor needs to attend an accredited course of study accompanied and followed by practical training and supervision. A counsellor needs to have an understanding of psychology and human developmental processes, understand counselling theory and a range of theoretical approaches. Additionally, a counsellor needs to work within a specific theoretical framework which either encompasses one model of practice or uses an integrative model of practice drawing on elements from a number of theoretical approaches. Counsellors use a range of skills and strategies appropriate for their model of practice.

Many counsellors work in a structured setting where people who are seeking counselling attend counselling sessions at specified times. Although other counsellors are more informal they usually have the expectation that the client will come to them to seek help.

Counselling is practised according to a set of standards and guidelines determined by professional bodies that set minimum accreditation standards and levels of competence. Counsellors are bound by codes of practice, which emphasise the counsellor's respect for the client's values, experience, thoughts, feelings and their capacity for self-determination. They aim to serve the best interests of a client (British Association for Counselling and Psychotherapy (BACP) *Guidelines for those Using Counselling Skills in their Work*, 1999). Additionally, counsellors are bound by ethical standards which stress the importance of boundaries in the relationship, particular qualities of the relationship and the specific goals of the counselling activity.

Boundaries in a counselling relationship

Counselling generally takes place in an environment where privacy can be ensured, and which provides for the physical and emotional safety of both the person being counselled and the counsellor. Information about the nature and purpose of the counselling relationship is clarified with the person being counselled, and rules relating to ethical boundaries are observed. For example, it is not acceptable for a counsellor to have affectionate physical contact with a client either during a counselling session or afterwards. Similarly, it is not appropriate for counsellors to make contact for their own personal reasons with people being counselled.

Qualities of a counselling relationship

The qualities of a relationship with a counsellor are different from the qualities of other kinds of relationship where counselling skills may be used in everyday life situations of either a social or work-related nature.

You might ask, 'What is different about the relationship between a counsellor and person being counselled and other relationships where counselling skills are used?' Perhaps the most important difference is that there is an unequal quality in the counsellor/ other person relationship. Counsellors put their own needs to one side and focus only on the needs of the other person. Of course, a friend or colleague can do this for while, but normally they will stay in touch with their own needs as well as the other person's needs. By contrast, a counsellor will usually put their own needs to one side while attending to the other person for the whole duration of the counselling session. A counsellor listens and focuses exclusively on the other person and their problems and does not intrude on the counselling process by talking about their own issues. This is obviously very different from a normal conversation between friends and workmates.

A counselling relationship does not include the normal reciprocal qualities of friendship. Counselling is a one-way process where the counsellor invites the other person to share their thoughts, feelings, experiences and problems, and the counsellor does little sharing except where this is for the direct benefit of the person being counselled. In contrast, friends share experiences mutually and this strengthens the bond between them.

A counselling relationship is most definitely not an authoritarian one. Counsellors strive to create an equal relationship with the people they are helping. This is very different from the relationship between supervisors and their staff in a work situation. In the work situation it is appropriate for a supervisor to give instructions, direction, and guidance to their staff so that company or agency policies are implemented and necessary goals and tasks are achieved. In this situation the relationship is certainly not an equal one, but it is still possible for the people involved to use counselling skills when appropriate.

Whereas people often try to persuade their friends to do the sort of things that they might do themselves, or to do things which they think are best, a counsellor behaves quite differently. A counsellor is somebody who encourages other people to do what they themselves want to do, instead of encouraging them to do what the counsellor thinks is best for them. This means that generally counsellors do not give advice.

Counsellors usually do not give advice or make suggestions about how to resolve problems from an expert point of view. Instead, they encourage the person being counselled to discover their own resources and solutions. By contrast, within a friendship, workmate, or supervisory relationship, even when counselling skills are being used, offering suggestions to the person in distress or difficulty may be useful, sensible, and appropriate.

Goals of counselling

Counselling usually involves helping people to address specific problems that are troubling them. Additionally, it often involves helping a person to develop different and more positive ways of coping with life. People seek counselling for a very wide range of purposes. Examples include: being emotionally distressed because of the loss of a loved one, feeling depressed and lonely, having relationship problems, suffering from stress, anxiety, and experiencing troubling thoughts as a result of past experiences. Often counselling will help people to develop skills and experience personal growth. Thus, resolving troubling issues or developing strengths to cope with life are common goals of counselling.

> **Counselling** is practised according to a set of standards and guidelines set by an appropriate professional body and in accordance with a code of practice which emphasises respect for the client's values, experience, thoughts, feelings and capacity for self-determination

The use of counselling skills

You don't need to be a counsellor to use the counselling skills that we will describe. These skills are certainly not limited to use by counsellors in counselling sessions. They are valuable communication skills which can be very effective in helping others when used in everyday conversation by people who are not counsellors.

Whenever a person is emotionally troubled, confused, having difficulty making a decision or solving a problem, the use of counselling skills can be helpful. For example, a neighbour might use counselling skills with the person next door who has recently separated from their partner. A medical practitioner might use counselling skills while treating a patient for injuries sustained during physical conflict with another person. An office worker might use counselling skills to help a colleague who is having trouble managing their workload. A teacher might use counselling skills to help a student talk about problems in studying.

Will the use of counselling skills change the relationship?

Everyday relationships are not the same as counsellor–client relationships and it is not appropriate for them to be the same.

Being a friend: If you have a friendship with someone they are unlikely to be appreciative if you try to behave as though you were their counsellor. Friendship is about mutuality, where each person shares equally in a relationship which is open and supportive. Your friend is likely to be appreciative though, if, when troubled, you can make it easier for them to talk to you about the things that are troubling them by using interpersonal skills such as listening and attending skills and other communication skills which will make it more comfortable for them to talk. In this process, unlike the counsellor, you will not be restrained by the counsellor's formal ethical boundaries and one-way relationship but instead can enjoy a normal friendship relationship. Thus, you will be free to talk about similar experiences you might have had and to share your own troubles with your friend. Depending on the sort of relationship you have, you may decide to put your arm round your friend or give them a hug in order to reassure or comfort them.

Being a manager: If you are a manager, your role naturally involves making decisions that affect others and having a level

9

of authority. Consequently, you cannot have the relationship that a counsellor has with their client. There will also be limits to the level of self-disclosure, which can appropriately be expected from a member of your staff. Even so, by using counselling skills appropriately you may be able to help a member of your staff to talk to you about problems that are troubling them, to help them make sensible decisions, and feel better. While doing this you need to recognise that your relationship is still a management one. It would not be appropriate to change role, but within the context of your role you can use counselling skills to make it easier for the other person to talk about those things that trouble them.

Being a nurse: If you are a nurse you will have a professional relationship with your patient which requires you to carry out particular medical procedures. While maintaining that relationship, which is quite different from a counsellor–client relationship, you may be able to help your patient feel better emotionally by using counselling skills.

You may notice in the examples we have given that the primary nature of the relationship between the person using counselling skills and the other person is substantially unchanged by the use of these skills. The friend relates as a friend, the manager relates as a manager, and the nurse relates as a nurse. It would be neither sensible nor appropriate to try to alter or disregard the nature of the primary relationship. However, although this relationship is substantially unchanged, in our experience, when people in any profession or social situation use counselling skills sensibly and appropriately, the relationship is enhanced.

Unlike the counselling situation, where direct advice is rarely given, counselling skills will sometimes be used in a context where it is both appropriate and necessary to provide information and/or give direct advice. Giving advice may at times help the person to solve problems and make decisions. This is particularly so where the person using counselling skills has knowledge or experience which the other person doesn't have. For example, a mother may use counselling skills while listening to her teenage daughter as she talks about a difficult relationship with her best girlfriend. The mother's primary role is as a parent, so, depending on the circumstances, it might be appropriate for her to make suggestions and/or give advice. Similarly a work supervisor may use counselling skills when addressing issues of punctuality with an employee who has recently returned to work following the birth of a new baby, and at the same time offer the employee advice based on current information about the company's policies regarding punctuality.

> Whenever we use **counselling skills** we need to recognise that we are intentionally communicating in a way that is different from general conversational dialogue

WHAT CAN WE ACHIEVE BY USING COUNSELLING SKILLS?

We wonder what ideas come into your mind when you ask yourself the question, 'What can we achieve by using counselling skills?' Would you like to stop and think about what you would like to achieve by using counselling skills? If so, we suggest that you complete the following:

I would like to use counselling skills to help people to:

1. ....

2. ....

3. ....

4. ....

We think that counselling skills can be used to comfort people in distress, and to help people with problems to:

● deal with their emotions so that they feel better
● deal with worrying thoughts and beliefs
● find solutions to problems
● make decisions

- feel more positive about themselves
- examine and maybe change their behaviours with regard to relationships with others.

Can you think back to a time when someone helped you by listening to you so that you could deal with troubling emotions or solve a difficult problem? If you can, then you are remembering an experience where someone probably, either deliberately or without realising what they were doing, used counselling skills to help you.

- What was that experience like?
- What were the most significant things that you still remember about that experience?
- Can you remember what it was like for you?
- Can you remember what that person did to help?

Our guess is that it might be easier for you to remember how you felt as a result of the experience, than for you to remember what the helper actually said or did. If the person used counselling skills it is quite possible that you hardly noticed what they were saying.

Although helping others using our communication skills is something that we learn to do throughout life and which we all do naturally, we can be more effective if we make use of some basic counselling skills.

CHOOSING WHEN, AND WHEN NOT, TO USE COUNSELLING SKILLS

Once you have improved your natural counselling skills you will be able to decide when to use them. For example, when relating to a friend you might playfully collude on a plan to encourage your partners to spend an evening out together or commiserate about the difficulties of raising teenage children. At other times you might decide that it is more important for you to focus on your friend's problems by using counselling skills for a while. If you do decide to make use of counselling skills, remember that you are still a friend, but you are choosing for a while to use particular communication skills to help your friend.

The decision about whether or not to use counselling skills in a conversation is an important one, which is best illustrated by use of an example.

David and the neighbour

Last week David met one of our neighbours, Julie. We have a friendly relationship with Julie and often have chats with her about the weather, friends, relatives, and things we are doing. However, last week as she started to talk about her son and daughter-in-law, David realised that she was becoming emotionally troubled. David then had to decide whether or not to use counselling skills to help her to feel better. In making this decision he had to take account of his relationship with Julie, the time available, the situation, and his own emotional energy.

David might have been in a hurry, might have realised that the situation was very public, or might have recognised that at that point in time he did not have the emotional resources to listen to someone else's problems. In taking into account any of these factors he might have decided that it was not appropriate to use counselling skills at that time. In this case, he might have said, 'I'm really sorry to hear that your son and daughter-in-law have problems. Young people often seem to find their relationships difficult in the early stages. I hope things will soon improve for them.' That would have been an appropriate, caring and friendly response. However, it would not have been a response that utilised counselling skills, because instead of inviting our neighbour to talk about how she felt, it would have effectively ignored her feelings, and closed the conversation on the subject by expressing the hope that things would improve.

As it happened, David didn't give this response, but instead chose to use counselling skills to help our neighbour express her emotions about the subject and to subsequently feel better as a result. By using counselling skills Julie was invited to talk in more detail about her worries. As a consequence, she talked at some length about her concerns and dealt with these in a way that seemed to be good for her.

It is important to recognise that by using counselling skills you will be either directly or indirectly giving the other person an invitation to talk to you about personal information. Thus, they may disclose information to you that is private and that they would prefer to be kept confidential. Therefore, when we use counselling skills we need to be sensitive to the other person's needs in this regard.

Whether or not you decide to use counselling skills will depend on several factors. It might be useful if you took a moment or two to think about the things that could influence your decision about whether or not to use them.

We think that the following questions are relevant:

- Can I provide a trusting relationship?
- Is the environment suitably private?
- Will I be able in my social or professional role to provide the required level of confidentiality?
- Am I feeling emotionally robust enough to listen to someone else's problems?
- Am I clear about my expectations regarding my relationship with the person and possible outcomes which may result from the conversation?
- Do I feel competent in inviting the person to discuss the problem in question?

Now that you have read this list you will probably realise that when we use counselling skills we have a moral obligation toward the person we are trying to help. If they choose to talk to us about sensitive and private issues we need to respect their confidentiality and make sure that other people can't overhear. The person we are talking with needs to be confident that they can trust us not to misuse the information they give us. These issues will be more fully discussed in Chapter 3.

In our previous example, because personal privacy is important, David was careful not to intrude and not to encourage the conversation to go further than our neighbour, Julie, might have wished. Because David was able to respect her limits she seemed to have a positive experience when talking with him. Additionally, because he did not try to encourage her to disclose more than she wished about her painful issues, she is likely to feel safe and comfortable when talking to him in the future.

Do you see the difference between using counselling skills in a conversation and just being a friend without using the skills? When we use counselling skills we invite the other person to talk more fully about their emotional feelings and thoughts in order to help them to feel better. When we use normal social communication skills we usually avoid doing this. Notice how it's possible to choose whether to use counselling skills or whether to respond in a different way, just as most friends would.

> You can choose whether or not to use counselling skills taking into account the relationship, the time available, the situation, and your own personal resources

Clearly, using counselling skills helps people to unload the burdens they are carrying by sharing problems in a way which enables them to deal with their emotional issues, make decisions, and feel better. Using counselling skills can also be satisfying for the person who uses them.

THE IMPACT ON YOU IF YOU USE COUNSELLING SKILLS

Although using counselling skills can be satisfying, we need to caution that there may be some level of emotional impact on anyone who chooses to use these skills. If you listen to other people as they talk about their emotional feelings and problems, there may be emotional consequences for you (see Chapters 5 and 10).

Let's go back to the example which we gave before, concerning our neighbour, Julie. When Julie started to tell David about her worries, she got in touch with some deep and painful emotions. As might be expected, because David is a person who is emotionally sensitive himself, the painful emotions which she was talking about triggered off similar, but less powerful, emotional feelings within him. Additionally, he was reminded of painful times in his own life. At some level it must have been painful for him to listen to her talk about her sadness, as she related her story. Thus, one of the costs of using counselling skills is that we are likely to be brought in touch with our own inner pain relating to our past and unresolved problems. Had David behaved like a typical neighbour and friend he might have said to Julie, 'I'm very sorry to hear that your son and daughter-in-law have problems and hope things will soon improve for them', and then changed the subject. By doing this he would have avoided listening to the neighbour's painful issues and would also have avoided having to face emotional pain himself.

If you decide to use counselling skills, then you need to be aware that you will be deliberately inviting people to talk about painful emotions and difficult problems. Consequently, you will have to face your own emotional responses to what they tell you. We are convinced that this is one of the reasons why the majority of the population put limits on their natural ability to use counselling skills. Most people have learnt smart ways of steering a conversation away from painful topics in order to protect themselves from the painfulness of listening to other people's problems. Instead of inviting a person to keep talking, people will commonly say things such as, 'Oh well, that's life', 'Never mind, things can only get better', or they may simply change the subject.

How many times have you heard someone say, 'I've got too many problems of my own to be bothered with other people's problems'? We might think that this is a very uncaring attitude. However, we believe that it is quite legitimate for a person to have this attitude. This is particularly so for people who lead stressful lives and have significant personal problems of their own. However, for us, the satisfaction which we receive as we help other people by using counselling skills is well worthwhile. We hope that the same will be true for you.

THE ADVANTAGES OF USING COUNSELLING SKILLS

From our experience, using counselling skills to help others can be very satisfying indeed. Through enabling other people to talk about and deal with their emotional experiences and to talk about and find solutions to their problems, it is possible to achieve considerable personal satisfaction. Our hope is that you will have similar positive experiences to ours.

Also, it is worth noting that if we are respectful of other people, and use our counselling skills sensitively, then our relationships with them may be enhanced, because they will find that they are able to relate to us in ways that are satisfying and meaningful for them.

EXPECTATIONS OF YOURSELF

If you are to have positive experiences when using counselling skills you will need to have a clear idea of your expectations of yourself. In order to help you to think further about your expectations, you might like to consider a practical example. Imagine that somebody called Michael comes to talk with you and tells you the following:

> During the last week, he has lost a job, which was very important to him. He has discovered that there is another job which he could have, but it's in a city which is six hours travelling time away from where he currently lives with his partner. His partner would not be able to go with him if he were to take the new job, and he is in a dilemma about what to do. He is also emotionally distressed because the job that he lost was very important to him.

Imagine that Michael went to school with you and that you play tennis with him regularly. While having a cup of coffee after your game of tennis today he has told you about his problem. He asks you for advice; should he take the new job or should he stay where he is without a job so that he can stay with his partner?

This example raises questions which apply to many situations in which the opportunity arises to use counselling skills as a way of helping. Perhaps you would like to stop reading for a minute to think about what expectations you might have of yourself in helping Michael.

We're going to list some possible expectations that we could have, and then think about whether they are realistic or not. Here they are:

1. I'll help him to find a job near where he and his partner live.
2. I'll talk to his partner and see if I can convince her to move with him.
3. I'll try to change his belief about needing to go to a new job.
4. I'll tell him to go to the new job and say that if his partner really loves him she will go with him.
5. I'll tell him that his relationship with his partner is more important than his job so he should stay with his partner.

What do you think of the above expectations?

Are you surprised when we say that we believe *all* of the expectations listed above are inappropriate and unrealistic! Can you guess why?

UNREALISTIC EXPECTATIONS WHEN USING COUNSELLING SKILLS

The expectations described are unrealistic for the following reasons:

1. If we expect that we can solve someone else's problems then we are being unrealistic and setting ourselves up for failure. Generally, it isn't possible to solve somebody else's problems. Every person has to solve their own problems. However, the use of counselling skills can facilitate the process needed for the person to be able to find their own solutions.

2. It is very difficult, if not impossible, to change someone else's beliefs or attitudes unless the person wants to change the way

they think. Trying to convince someone to think differently, or to do something they really don't want to do, will not work.

3. It is often sensible to avoid giving advice even when asked for it. Of course, there are many exceptions to this rule in everyday life.

Giving advice – is it sensible or not?

The question of whether or not to give advice can be a difficult one and is very dependent on the context in which the advice is sought. There are many situations in everyday life where it is sensible and appropriate to give advice. For example consider the following:

● If, as a paramedic, a person phones you in a very distressed state to tell you that their son has just fallen off a ladder and is unconscious, obviously it would be essential for you to give some clear advice in order to save the young person's life.

● You are in a management position and know that what one of your staff is doing will lead to negative consequences. You therefore have a responsibility to give advice.

● You are a teacher and a student asks you about job opportunities which could arise if they were to undertake particular courses of study. You may wish to give factual information and advice about career options.

Clearly, there are limitless examples of situations where giving advice is the smart thing to do. However, there are many everyday situations in which it is not smart to give advice. We will explain why, but before we do we suggest that you might want to take a minute or two to think about why giving advice is often unhelpful. What ideas do you have?

How do the reasons you have thought of compare with our list?

● If you give advice, the advice may fit for you but not for the other person. The other person may reject the advice or may be unable to act on it. Either way, that person will not be left feeling good because having talked with you they have not accepted your advice.

- The person may take your advice and it may result in a positive outcome. Although this may help you to feel good, the danger is that the person concerned will believe that you are a wise person who needs to be consulted whenever difficult decisions are to be made. In effect you will have taken away the person's confidence in their ability to make decisions for themselves.

- The person may take the advice and it may result in a negative outcome. In this case the person is likely to be justifiably angry with you!

We need to accept that people with problems will commonly ask those they trust for advice. Sometimes a person will ask for advice by saying something like, 'What would you do?' or, 'I don't know what to do. What do you think I should do?' When faced with questions like these, we suggest that you respond directly and make it clear that it is more important for the person concerned to do what is right for them rather than to do what might fit for you. For example you might respond by saying something like:

I think that what's most important is for you to do what is right for you. What options do you have?

Of course, the person might respond by saying, 'I don't know, and that's why I'm asking you what to do.' In which case you might respond with:

I don't know what the best solution is for you. But, if we keep talking about it we might discover some options.

It may also be helpful to let the person know that what they are trying to figure out is difficult and possibly confusing.

> Giving advice can only help the person to solve problems and make decisions if you are able to offer accurate and up-to-date information which relates directly to their current situation

REALISTIC EXPECTATIONS

When we use counselling skills we need to make sure that the person we're trying to help doesn't have unrealistic expectations of us. Similarly we need to be careful not to set expectations of ourselves which are unrealistically high.

Recognising your limits

Be kind to yourself by being realistic about how much you can help another person. At times you may ask yourself, 'Can I help this person?'. If you are unsure, remember that you can always suggest that they talk to someone else who is more qualified to help. We all have limits to what we can do to help others. Consequently, we need to have a clear understanding of the limits to our own personal commitment to helping others. There will be times when you will recognise that more expert, or specialist, help is needed, and will recommend that the person you are helping should talk to someone else who is better qualified. Referring a person for help to someone who has appropriate qualifications and training is a responsible and appropriate course of action in situations where you realise that you do not have the expertise required. Recognition of our own limits is essential if we are to be responsible when trying to help others.

> Recognise your limitations so that you know when to refer someone you want to help to a person who has the required qualifications, training and experience

Setting realistic expectations

We think that realistic expectations include:

1. Trying to create a trusting, caring relationship with the person seeking help.

2. Actively listening to the person's story, so that the person feels heard and understood.
3. Trying to recognise and acknowledge the person's emotional feelings and allowing them to talk about these.
4. Trying to help the person to sort out their confusion and resolve troubling issues.
5. Providing the person with an opportunity to consider solutions to problems, to consider alternatives and to make decisions which fit for them.

What other expectations might you add to this list?

Are they realistic?

Hopefully, the outcome of helping a person will be that they will feel better emotionally. Additionally they may be able to resolve issues, find solutions to problems and make beneficial decisions. It would be great if these things were always achieved, but to expect that this will necessarily happen is unrealistic.

Sometimes you may discover that inviting a person to talk to you by using counselling skills results in them getting in touch with strong emotions which leave them in a disturbed state. If this happens, it is responsible and sensible to suggest to them that they seek help from a suitably qualified person.

We believe that the most important expectation, which certainly can be achieved, is for you to listen in a caring and respectful way so that the person seeking help knows that someone has heard what they have to say and has recognised the painfulness of their situation. If you can do this, you will be performing a very useful service and are likely to gain a sense of personal satisfaction.

chapter summary

■ In order to help other people we need to listen and communicate with them in ways that enable them to share their troubles and feel better.

■ We need to listen in a caring and respectful way so that the person concerned knows that someone has heard what they have to say and has recognised the painfulness of their situation.

■ Basic counselling skills can be used in everyday conversation to help people to talk about their problems and emotional feelings, and to make decisions.

■ Using basic counselling skills is not the same as counselling, so we all need to recognise our limitations and refer to qualified counsellors when appropriate.
  ● You can choose when, and when not, to use counselling skills.
  ● We need to have realistic expectations of ourselves.
  ● There are disadvantages in giving advice although in some situations this is essential and/or desirable.

■ Using counselling skills can be emotionally demanding, but satisfying.

ASSIGNMENT EXERCISES FOR COURSEWORK STUDENTS

1. Think about a time in the past when you have helped someone else who had a problem. Describe the things that you did and the ways you behaved which you think were helpful to the other person. Also describe things that you did and ways that you behaved that might not have been helpful to the other person.

2. Describe situations which arise in either your professional or social life where you believe that the use of counselling skills would be helpful. Explain what you would hope to achieve for the other person and for yourself by using such helping skills.

3. When we are trying to help other people it is important for us to recognise our limits. Discuss, using practical examples to illustrate your answer, how you will recognise that you have reached the limit of your ability to help and thus need to suggest that the person seeking help should consult with someone who has more expertise.

2 Valuing the person

As we have explained previously, helping another person requires the use of particular listening and communication skills. Additionally, it is dependent on the kind of relationship you are able to establish with that person. When using counselling skills the relationship between you and the other person is a special relationship. It needs to have special qualities if the counselling skills you use are to be of most help.

THE PERSON-CENTRED APPROACH

Many years ago, Carl Rogers developed an approach to counselling which is now usually referred to as the person-centred approach. Initially, Rogers called it the client-centred approach, but later realised that it was important to treat the individual he was helping as a person rather than as a client.

Rogers' assumptions were that people were essentially trustworthy, had positive inner qualities, and had the potential for understanding themselves and resolving their own problems. Consequently, he believed that the helper did not need to directly intervene or provide solutions as the other person was capable of doing this themselves.

> People have the potential to find their own solutions

Rogers emphasised that the attitudes and personal characteristics of the helper and the quality of the helper's relationship with the other person were central in determining the outcome of any helping conversation.

Rogers disputed many of the traditional beliefs about counselling. He challenged the usefulness of giving advice, making suggestions, pointing people in a particular direction, persuading, teaching and interpreting the thoughts and feelings of others. Additionally, he believed that it was important when helping other people, to avoid sharing a great deal about yourself, and instead to focus on the other person's story by reflecting and clarifying their verbal and non-verbal communication.

It is interesting to note that since Rogers first put forward his ideas, research has consistently supported his belief that the helping relationship contributes more than any other factor to a positive outcome for the person being helped.

> The relationship is more important than the problem

Rogers believed that the helping process not only enabled people to discover solutions to their own problems but also enabled them to experience personal growth so that they would be able to cope more effectively with problems in the future.

> The person is more important than the solution

The basic principles of the person-centred approach are very suitable for use in many situations which arise in everyday life. They enable informal and unstructured helping conversations to take place in almost any situation. The approach is non-intrusive and respectful of the other person. That person is treated as an equal who is quite capable of finding their own solutions.

WHY DO YOU WANT TO HELP OTHER PEOPLE?

Because you are reading this book we assume that you are interested in helping other people to feel better and to cope in a more comfortable way with the struggles that life brings. Have you ever thought about your reasons for wanting to help others? Would you like to take a minute or two to jot down your reasons for wanting to help other people?

I want to help people because:

1. ....

2. ....

3. ....

There are many reasons why people feel drawn to caring about and helping other people. However, it is worth looking at your reasons because these can affect the way in which you provide help. For example, it may be that you believe that because of your own life experiences you have the answers to many common dilemmas that confront other people. It is certainly true that it may make it easier for you to join with other people and to understand their responses to their difficulties if you have experienced similar problems. Even so, there is danger in assuming that your own experiences and responses will be exactly the same as someone else's. What is worse is that if we try to impose our own solutions on someone else they may not fit, so we may unintentionally intensify their own feelings of confusion, frustration, and helplessness. Additionally, we effectively disempower them by negating their ability to find their own solutions. On the other hand, if we value the uniqueness of the person we're trying to help, instead of drawing from our own experience, we will enable them to find from within themselves the solutions which suit them best.

You may wish to enhance your ability to help other people by learning some counselling skills because helping others is a strong value of yours. Thus by learning new ways of helping you can satisfy your need to preserve that value and can feel more fulfilled as a person by doing so.

Thinking about our values, needs, attitudes and experiences can shed some light on what it is we're getting from helping others. Sometimes having the experience of being helped ourselves can increase our level of self-awareness with regard to our motives for wanting to help others. Additionally, opportunities for simple self-exploration and reflection can help us understand why it is important for us to help others.

Many people are motivated to help other people by a desire to be liked, appreciated, and respected. All the motivations we have described are valid and useful. However, what we need to do is to ensure that our motivations do not intrude on the value of our helpfulness. We can do this if we take the time to think about our motivations and discover how these might influence the way that we help other people. If you have difficulty doing this you may wish to talk with a counsellor about the issues involved for you. Although we are both professional counsellors ourselves, we find that it is useful for us to talk to another counsellor at times. This provides us with the opportunity to resolve our personal issues, undergo personal growth, and try to minimise the influence of our own issues when we are trying to help someone else.

The influence of Monica's issues

Monica is a woman in middle age. She must be somewhere in her mid- to late fifties. She had been successfully running a small business with her long-term partner, Doug. Sadly, Doug contracted a terminal illness and, as she needed to care for him, Monica closed the business. Doug eventually died early last year. As well as overcoming her grief, Monica started to feel lonely and unproductive. After a while she decided to actively help other people by working in her local 'Opportunity' shop. Monica has a high level of personal insight and realised that because of her loneliness she was actively trying to engage people who came into the shop in lengthy conversations rather than respecting their personal needs. After talking with a counsellor about this issue she enrolled in a course designed to help her use counselling skills in the conversations she entered into while working at the shop. She says that she always needs to be aware of her loneliness issue and consequent need for human contact. In her work at the shop she is now able to help other people who are troubled without trying to engage them in unnecessarily long conversations. Additionally, she has taken some steps to improve her social life so that, while still missing Doug, she is able, to some degree, to satisfy her need for company.

> Our own personal issues will influence the effectiveness of the help we offer other people

Sometimes, when we try to help others, the things they tell us trigger off past memories so that old emotional wounds of our own are reopened. A common response to this is for helpers to use strategies which deflect the other person away from their painful issue. Thus, instead of helping a person to continue talking we may be inclined to try to 'cheer them up'. Although we may try to fool ourselves into thinking otherwise, in reality we do this to prevent them from continuing to talk about the matters that remind us of our own painful experiences. It therefore follows that if we are to be helpful to other people it is sensible for us to try to resolve our own issues so that our own wounds are healed. A good way to do this is with the help of a counsellor.

HELPFUL ATTITUDES AND CHARACTERISTICS

Can you think of a time when you were troubled and someone listened to you in a helpful way? Can you remember how the person who was helping you related to you? Was there anything special about the relationship you had with the person at the time? If there was, you might like to jot down some notes.

What was special about the relationship was:

1. ....

2. ....

3. ....

As we pointed out earlier, most people would agree that the relationship between a helper and the person being helped is the central ingredient in determining the effectiveness of the helping process. It has been conclusively shown that the personal qualities of helpers are significant in contributing to positive growth. Additionally, it has been found that the beliefs, values and traits of people who are effective in helping others are markedly different from those of people who are not effective when trying to help others. It is therefore important for us to ask the question, 'What are the most useful characteristics of a helping relationship?'. We will base our answer to this question on the ideas first proposed by Carl Rogers.

Rogers identified three primary characteristics which he considered to be essential when helping others. These were congruence, empathy, and unconditional positive regard. He also talked about the need to treasure the helping relationship and the person being helped. In our discussion of attitudes and characteristics that are useful when helping others we will use the acronym TREASURE to suggest that for effective outcomes the relationship must contain the following elements:

Trust
Respect
Empathy
Acceptance
Safety
Unconditional
Real
Expert.

Trust

If we are to be successful in helping someone we clearly need to have their trust. Without this, they are certainly not going to feel free to talk to us about intimate personal problems. Additionally, is very unlikely that they will get in touch with their emotional feelings in a way which will allow them to express these so that they can feel better.

Gaining a person's trust is a complex process which will be coloured by the person's experience of us both in the past and in the present. It is also dependent on the situation and the fundamental nature of the relationship. Clearly, the issue of trust will be affected by the perceived agendas of both the person being helped and the helper. To illustrate this we will tell you about Simon.

Simon

Simon is a young man in his early 20s. A while ago he made the mistake of relying on the use of illegal drugs in order to cope with the pressures of his life. As a consequence he got heavily into debt and recently became worried because he believed that the people he owed money to were both unscrupulous and violent. One of Simon's workmates, Damien, was worried about Simon because he could see that he was troubled. Damien has very strong and rather inflexible religious beliefs and disapproves of drug use. When Damien approached Simon to invite him to talk, Simon initially found it very difficult to trust him. He suspected that Damien's agenda was to try to convert him to Damien's religious beliefs, although in fact this was not true.

Can you see how difficult it was for Simon to trust Damien, and how hard it would be for Damien to convince Simon that it was safe to talk with him? As we will discuss later, Damien did succeed in gaining Simon's trust and was consequently able to help him sort out his problem.

Respect

Respect involves valuing the person for who they are as a person, respecting and valuing their ability to find solutions to their own problems, and having a positive attitude to them based on the belief that regardless of what they have done, they are doing the best that they can. Respect involves believing that the person being helped has the ability to take charge of their own life and undergo personal growth, and has the potential to be a positive influence in the world. In short, respect involves treasuring the person for what they are and treating them as someone to be valued.

> Respect involves treating the person as someone to be valued

Respecting someone may sound very easy, but sometimes it is not. If you think back to the case of Simon and Damien, you may recognise that because of their different lifestyles and beliefs it may have been difficult for Damien to respect Simon. It was only because Damien was able to do this, and to communicate his respect to Simon, that Simon was able to start relating to Damien in a way which enabled positive outcomes to occur.

Empathy

We are sure that you won't be surprised to hear that for positive outcomes you will need to create a positive, warm, and caring relationship between yourself and the person being helped. Carl Rogers used the word 'empathy' to describe this attribute of a helping relationship. As a consequence of his influence, the words 'empathy' and 'empathic' have become rather jargonistic. Although generally we prefer not to use jargon, the word 'empathy' is extremely useful because it encapsulates the idea of being able to fully understand and share another person's feelings, and in doing so almost to let go of one's own sense of identity in joining with the other person.

> Empathy involves fully understanding and sharing another person's feelings

Some people talk about an empathic relationship metaphorically by describing the listener as walking in the other person's shoes. Sometimes, while someone is sharing personal information, it can be useful to try to imagine what you would see and how you would feel if you were in that person's shoes and were looking at their situation from their vantage point. If you do this, you will be able to imagine and understand their world and, to some extent, identify with them.

If the relationship is warm, caring and empathic, then the person being helped will feel valued and safe about sharing intimate personal information. Such a relationship enables the helper to more fully understand the other person's point of view, and to correctly identify that person's emotional feelings. Further, if the helper joins with the other person and imagines what it would be like to be them, then they will inevitably experience similar emotional feelings.

Acceptance

We have previously talked about valuing the other person. Part of being able to value them involves accepting who they are. Paradoxically, if we are able to accept the person as they are, we have the best chance of joining with them in a way which will enable them to change, grow, and develop into the person they wish to become. The opposite of being accepting is to be critical. Have you noticed that when you are critical of someone they will generally resist changing and become more entrenched in their thinking and behaviours. When we accept them, they feel valued, are able to feel good about themselves, they can get in touch with positive parts of their personality, and move forward to achieve gains for themselves.

Damien had no illusions about Simon. He knew who he was. But he was able to accept him and, as a consequence, Simon was able to make decisions for himself which resulted in significant change and positive growth.

Safety

If we are to be helpful to someone we need to create a relationship and environment where they are able to talk freely. They will not be able to talk with us freely unless they feel safe in doing so. Initially, in his relationship with Damien, Simon was worried about talking freely about his use of illegal drugs. He didn't feel safe. He was worried that Damien might decide to report him to the authorities. Clearly, the issue of safety is related to the issue of trust. As trust developed between Damien and Simon, Simon began to feel safe and was able to talk more freely about his real situation.

Unconditional

To be most helpful the relationship with the person you're helping needs to be unconditional. If it is conditional on your expectations of them, then your ability to help them will be seriously compromised.

Carl Rogers suggested that the helper needed to have 'unconditional positive regard'. By this he meant that the helper needed to unconditionally accept the other person and to see them in a positive light. Unconditionally accepting a person involves being non-judgemental. We have to recognise that this is not always possible, but it is certainly a goal we should strive for if we are to be as helpful as possible to others. The problem is that if we sit in judgement on the other person we will compromise our relationship with them, and because they feel judged they may become defensive rather than being open in exploring their issues with us.

> Unconditional acceptance involves being non-judgemental

How are we to achieve the difficult task of trying to be non-judgemental? What we need to do is to try to visualise the world *as it is seen* by the other person. Their world is coloured by their values, attitudes and beliefs and not ours. To enter into their world might be difficult for us. We may find ourselves making judgements about their attitudes, beliefs and values. However, we need to try to put these judgements to one side so that the person we are helping has the opportunity to deal with their emotional distress.

In order to be effective helpers, while we are listening we need to try to avoid making judgements about what we believe to be right or wrong, and instead focus on trying to see the world as the other person sees it. If you don't do this, then the other person is likely to feel judged and to stop talking freely. Their anxiety and sense of distress will rise and they will be less able to confront their troubling issues in a way which is satisfying for them.

Perhaps it would be useful to consider a specific example where beliefs and values could interfere with a helper's effectiveness. Imagine the following:

> You are a mother with a child who attends a day-care centre. You have noticed that one of the other children who attends the

33

centre is aggressive towards other children. While talking to the child's mother she tells you that the child's behaviour is deteriorating. The child throws tantrums and is extremely rude and disrespectful, with the consequence that the mother is distraught and at her wits' end with regard to how to manage the child. As the conversation progresses you discover that the child's mother frequently uses physical punishment.

This is a good example of a situation where many people have strong beliefs. Some people believe that any form of physical punishment is abuse and not acceptable. Other people believe that the physical punishment of children, provided that it isn't excessive, is not only appropriate but also necessary.

Imagine that you are someone who believes that the use of physical punishment is wrong. It might be tempting for you to interrupt the conversation by talking about the rights and wrongs of using physical punishment for controlling behaviour. Do you think that this would be useful?

If you were to raise your concerns regarding the use of physical punishment you would be satisfying your immediate needs instead of the needs of the mother who wanted help. You would certainly move her away from talking about her problems and her distress. She would feel judged and would be less likely to be open with you from then on. However, if you were to encourage her to continue talking about her own issues without interruption, then it might emerge that she was worried about the change in her relationship with her child. She might be able to address her concerns about how to deal with the child more effectively, and might even get in touch with feelings of inadequacy as a parent, but without feeling criticised.

This doesn't mean that you should condone behaviour of which you don't approve, or appear to agree with beliefs which are different from your own. What it does mean is that you should put your own values and beliefs to one side *while the person is talking about their issues and problems*. In the example given, it might be that later, when the emotional problems have been addressed, you will have an opportunity to raise the possibility that the mother might want to look at alternative ways of parenting. At this point she may be ready to do this, having recognised that the methods she has been using have not worked.

If it were to emerge that unacceptable levels of physical punishment were occurring (once again, we hit a values question – what is acceptable?) then you may find that you will need to make a decision with regard to ensuring the physical safety of the child. However, for an optimal outcome to occur, confrontation about this issue would be more usefully addressed after the mother has had an opportunity to talk openly and in a non-threatening climate about her own emotional issues. Later in this chapter we will discuss the issue of confidentiality and the need to deal with disclosing information at times, because we do have a duty to ensure the protection of children from all forms of abuse.

Can you see how an *uncritical* and *non-judgemental* acceptance of the other person, regardless of their values and beliefs, can enable them to feel valued, and enable you, the helper, to join with them, and most importantly give them an invitation to talk freely and openly without restraint? Thus a relationship of trust can develop.

As you have been reading this section you may have recognised that it will be very difficult at times to be unconditionally accepting and non-judgemental, important though this is to the helping process. It is certainly not always easy to do this because we all have beliefs and values and these may sometimes be different from those of the person we are helping.

When you engage in a helping conversation, you may discover that the person you are talking with has attitudes, beliefs and values which are different from yours. How do you think this will affect your ability to help this person to work through their problems? You could try to persuade them that your values and beliefs are better than theirs, and that they should accept them. Do you think this would be helpful? From our own experience as helpers, we can say that generally it is not helpful. The person-centred approach of unconditional, non-judgemental acceptance is far more likely to have success. This issue, of differences in beliefs and values, is an important one for spiritual leaders and culturally diverse people who have strong belief systems which are central to their lives. Such people need to be true to themselves so we will now discuss the issues involved in being 'real'.

Real

When we are helping someone we need to be real, genuine and, as Rogers said, 'congruent'. This inevitably raises the question, 'Do you think that you will be the same or different, when you are helping someone, from the person you are at other times?' What do you think?

It might be tempting for some people to try to change their personalities when helping others. People who try to do this are rarely successful as helpers. This is because the people being helped are unlikely to be duped, and likely to see through the charade, as the person trying to help them pretends to be somebody they are not. If you are to help someone, it is essential that they should be able to trust you. They will not be able to trust you if you pretend to be different from who you really are and they sense that you are not genuine. Thus, when you help someone you need to be authentically yourself. If you are not, you will not present yourself as congruent and, as a consequence, the person you are trying to help will not be able to trust you.

> Be yourself

We all have our own values, beliefs and attitudes, and these affect the way we live and behave. These values, beliefs and attitudes will also affect the way we feel about other people and the way we judge their behaviour. We all make decisions about what is right and what is wrong, and sometimes we feel strongly about those decisions. You can probably recognise that your friends do not all think alike on all matters. We are all different. For example, some people have strong ideas about the importance of family life, but others see things differently and place more importance on the individual than on the family.

As a helper you need to be true to your own values and beliefs. However, you will also need to avoid letting your own values and beliefs interfere with your ability to join with the person you are helping, and see the world in the way that they see it.

To be a successful helper you will need to bring your whole self into the relationship, including your personality, skills, attitudes and beliefs. By doing this you will be seen as a real person, genuine, congruent and trustworthy.

While being clear about your own attitudes and beliefs, it is very important to try to avoid imposing these onto the other person. That would not be appropriate, and would certainly not be helpful.

If you bring your whole self into a helping situation you will feel complete rather than fragmented. Thus, your behaviour as a helper will fit with the rest of you, and the person you are helping will perceive you as genuine and be able to trust you.

Expert

We do not see ourselves as experts on solving other people's problems, so why do we see the quality of 'being expert' as so important when helping other people? What we believe to be important is for the person we are helping to see themselves as the expert. Additionally, as helpers, we think it is essential for us to recognise that the people we are helping have the inner resources themselves to work through their problems and find their own solutions. They are the experts when it comes to understanding themselves and discovering ways to feel better. We are not the experts in this regard, they are.

> The person you are helping is the expert on finding solutions to their own problems

It follows that when we are trying to help someone to sort through their problems, rather than struggling to find solutions for them, we need to respect their ability and their own resources. Thus we rely on them to use their own initiative in seeking and putting into place solutions to their problems. What we do as helpers is merely facilitate this process.

CONFIDENTIALITY

If we are to value the person we are helping then we need to be able to respect their need for confidentiality. If we are not able to do that people will not share openly with us, as they may fear repercussions. It is therefore often sensible and useful to say, somewhere near the beginning of the conversation, that what is being said will be treated confidentially. For example, you might say:

I'd like you to know that what you tell me will be treated confidentially and I will keep what you say to myself, but if you want to talk to someone else about what we discuss, that's fine.

Notice the suggestion that the person being helped might want to talk to someone else later. Sometimes, the person being helped will find it useful to chat informally to another person in order to tie up loose ends.

Limits to confidentiality

In practice, there will sometimes be limits to the level of confidentiality that can be provided. It is important for you to recognise where limits to confidentiality occur, so that you can ensure the safety of others and yourself.

What would you do if someone told you that he intended to murder his wife? Would you treat the information confidentially? Of course you wouldn't. The only responsible and ethical response to this information would be to ensure that the person threatened was fully protected. Clearly there are issues regarding the extent to which confidentiality can be maintained. If you are told things which can't ethically be kept confidential, then you will need to decide when and how to tell the person that you do need to disclose the information to someone else. This could sometimes raise a dilemma for you as a helper. If you are not able to offer some level of confidentiality to the person you are helping, they are unlikely to openly share information which may be troubling them. However, we do need to be responsible where issues of safety are concerned.

Another impediment to the provision of confidentiality is that in most countries, for people who belong to particular professions, there are legal requirements which make it mandatory to report certain behaviours. For example, where we live, in Queensland, medical practitioners and teachers are legally mandated to report any suspicion of sexual abuse to the authorities. Although as counsellors, in our state, there is no legal requirement for us to do this, we still have an ethical obligation.

Dealing with the need to disclose information

It may be useful for you to examine your attitudes about disclosing information where issues of safety or risk of harm or abuse are involved. If you find that you need to disclose information, how will you do that? Will you let the person know that you need to disclose information which they have given you? If you don't let them know, you must accept that you are breaking their trust, but sometimes you will be wise to do this for your own safety. Personally, we prefer to be open about what we intend to do when we judge that it is safe to do so, but this is not always the case. If there is a risk to your safety, protect yourself and pass on the information discreetly.

MAINTAINING ETHICAL PRINCIPLES

Because of the caring and empathic relationship that will develop between you and a person being helped, it is essential to recognise the need for clear boundaries. Although you need to join effectively with the person, there also need to be clear limits to the closeness of the relationship. Without these limits the effectiveness of your assistance will be diminished. This is particularly true if you are using counselling skills in your job as a team leader or line manager and are also responsible for meeting certain objectives of the organisation or agency for which you work.

When you begin to get too close to the people you are helping you are likely to lose the ability to stand back objectively and assess what needs to happen for your conversation to be helpful. It may sound contradictory to suggest that the relationship should be warm, empathic and caring, and then say that you need to stand back and to be objective. Certainly, these two things are quite different, because one involves closeness and the other involves distance, and you can't do both at the same time.

We have observed that it is helpful to continually alternate between doing two different things. First, and most importantly, it is essential to be able to join effectively with the other person and to create a relationship which is warm, caring and empathic. Second though, it is valuable to be able to move back mentally and emotionally, from time to time, as the conversation proceeds. This distancing is needed to enable you to gain an overview of the other person's situation, and an overview of the conversation, so that your responses continue to be fitting and helpful.

Do you think that you can create a warm empathic relationship and at the same time move back from time to time to make decisions about how you need to respond? In practice this is not too hard. If you learn to focus primarily on the empathic relationship, then it will become apparent to you when you need to move back, and you will soon find that you can do this naturally and spontaneously.

There is another important reason for setting clear boundaries and this is related to the inequality of the helping relationship.

Is the helping relationship an equal or unequal relationship?

Do you think that the relationship between you and the person you are helping should be equal or unequal? Well, in some ways there is equality, and in other ways inequality. Clearly, both people need to be respected and valued. Neither one is superior or inferior to the other.

If the person being helped thinks that the helper is superior to themselves they may feel powerless to make their own decisions. They may, as a result, believe that they are incapable of solving their own problems and that they will always need someone else to help. However, if they are encouraged to accept that they are not only equally as competent and capable as the person they are talking with, but are also the expert when it comes to understanding themselves, then they are more likely to feel able to take control of their life and make sensible decisions.

Although there needs to be respect and a sense of equality between the helper and the person being helped, the relationship is in some ways unequal. It's unequal because the person being helped is being invited to share their issues and troubling problems, but the opposite does not usually happen. While helping another person it is not appropriate or useful for you to use the conversation to sort out your own problems, or even to share similar experiences in detail, as this would be distracting. Doing this may also contribute to the other person's feelings of inadequacy and incompetence as they may recognise that they have been unable to do what you have done. Consequently, the communication in a helping conversation, with regard to the sharing of painful issues, will often be primarily a one-way process. At other times, limited disclosure of information about yourself that is similar to that expressed by the other person can help them to have positive feelings about themselves and their situation.

> The helper listens – the person being helped talks

Because of the unequal nature of the relationship, it is likely that people being helped will see you as a person who doesn't have problems, who is sensible and mature, warm and caring and a person who should be greatly admired. Unless we have delusions of grandeur, we must admit that such a view is unrealistic as it hides the less attractive facets of our personalities. Unfortunately, troubled people who accept help in talking through their problems are often susceptible to offers of friendship. It is therefore important to set boundaries so that they are not seduced into relationships which are inappropriate, and don't form unrealistic dependencies or attachments.

As we mentioned in Chapter 1, professional counsellors are guided by a code of ethics.

Counselling is practised according to a set of standards and guidelines drawn up by professional bodies that determine minimum accreditation standards and levels of competence. Counsellors are bound by codes of practice which emphasise the counsellor's respect for the client's values, experiences, thoughts, feelings and their capacity for self-determination (British Association for Counselling and Psychotherapy (BACP), *Guidelines for those Using Counselling Skills in their Work*, 1999). Additionally, counsellors are bound by ethical standards which stress the importance of boundaries in the relationship, particular qualities of the relationship and specific goals of the counselling activity.

You may notice that the guidelines for counsellors set down by the BACP include not only counsellors, but also those people who use counselling skills in their work. When using counselling skills in everyday life you also need to ensure that you comply with guidelines such as those provided by the BACP.

Here are some questions to help you evaluate your ethical standards:

- In what way is my behaviour self-serving?
- Am I preoccupied with helping a particular person at work and if so what is my motive?
- Would I like to see much more of this person than is appropriate?
- Am I imposing values and suggestions that are not consistent with this person's cultural background?
- Am I beginning to dislike/become attracted to/become responsible for this person because they remind me of my mother/father/last partner?
- Am I beginning to become frustrated with this person because they won't take my advice?
- Am I at risk of inadvertently hurting this person?
- Am I choosing the direction of the conversations with this person or are they?
- Am I able to honour my original commitment to this person?
- If I continue to help this person will I become involved in an activity which reflects a conflict of interest?
- Am I beginning to view this person as helpless/irresponsible/hopeless/incompetent/manipulative and so on?

If your answers to the questions above suggest that you may be at risk of infringing appropriate ethical standards, we strongly suggest that you talk to a counsellor. By doing this you will have the opportunity to deal with the relevant personal issues for yourself and make informed decisions with regard to any action you need to take to ensure ongoing ethical behaviour.

UNDERSTANDING AND RESPECTING DIFFERENCE

As helpers, if we are to value the people we assist, we need to understand and respect differences related to race, culture, gender, sexuality, spirituality, age and disability. If you are to be an effective helper you will need to think about the way such differences influence you when you are talking to people from backgrounds that are different from your own. It is important for us to discover and own our prejudices because these are sure to influence the way we talk with people from backgrounds which are different from our own.

When trying to help a person from another background, it can be helpful to remember:

- That it is not necessary for me to know everything about the person's background for me to help them. I can ask them about things that I do not understand.
- To recognise the common ground that I share with the person.
- That it is not necessary for me to have had the same experiences as the person.
- That I can help this person if I take the time to understand their behaviour.

In order to understand difference and diversity we need to understand how our own heritage, culture and background influences our beliefs, attitudes and values. We then need to recognise the ways in which we respond to people who have different backgrounds from ours. We strongly suggest that readers take time to complete the assignment examples at the end of this chapter. Those readers who are learning counselling skills for use in everyday life as part of an organised course might benefit by discussing these assignment examples in a group setting with other students.

chapter summary

■ The relationship is the most important factor in producing a positive outcome.

■ Our own issues are certain to influence our helping behaviour, so we need to be aware of them and resolve them.

■ Characteristics of the helping relationship fit the acronym TREASURE:
- T for trust which needs to be established.
- R for respect for the person being helped.
- E for empathy.
- A for acceptance of the person as a person of value.
- S for safety in disclosing information.
- U for unconditional acceptance involving a non-judgemental attitude.
- R for real; the helper needs to be real, authentic, genuine and congruent.
- E for expert: the person being helped has the expertise to find their own solutions to their problems.

■ Confidentiality is desirable but there are limits to the extent of confidentiality which can be given in some situations.

■ It is essential to maintain ethical principles.

■ We need to understand and respect difference.

ASSIGNMENT EXERCISES FOR COURSEWORK STUDENTS

1. As well as having your own values and beliefs about various issues you will also carry with you your own heritage, traditions and customs. Discuss the way your social and cultural conditioning has influenced you, and the way that it influences the decisions you make.

2. Some of the people you meet will have come from backgrounds that are different from yours. Make a list of some social/cultural backgrounds that are different from yours:

a. . . . .

b. . . . .

c. . . . .

d. . . . .

Choose one of the above and briefly describe how you think this cultural background may be different from yours with regard to:

Treatment of the elderly
Child-rearing practices
Illness, disability, trauma and death
Expression of emotion
Gender relationships.

Discuss how these differences might hinder your conversation with someone from that background.

3. The second step in the process of recognising diversity and how you will interact with those from diverse backgrounds is to examine how society, your local community, and you yourself respond to those beliefs, practices and behaviours which are different from your own. From the list below tick those responses, which *your community* might choose as ways of reacting to others from different backgrounds:

Being oppressive
Being respectful
Being coercive
Being dominating
Responding with fear
Stereotyping
Integrating.

List 6 other ways:

a. . . . .

b. . . . .

c. . . . .

d. . . . .

e. . . . .

f. . . . .

From the combined list put a cross next to those responses which *you* might choose as ways of reacting to others from diverse backgrounds. Do you notice any differences? How will you let the person you are helping know that you are different and that you would like to understand them?

4. We would be deceiving ourselves if we assumed that our own experiences, beliefs and values did not influence our relationships with others. Explore this issue by answering *one* of the following questions:

   a. How would your values influence your ability to help a person involved in a gay relationship, if you yourself were heterosexual, or to help a person in a heterosexual relationship if you yourself were gay? Would you be inclined to direct them towards a different lifestyle or would you be able to fully accept them and help them to meet their personal goals? How would you develop a relationship of trust?

   b. Identify your own religious or spiritual belief system, or lack of belief system. What impact would this have on a helping conversation you had with an atheist, an agnostic, or a person with fundamentalist religious beliefs (different from yours if you hold fundamentalist beliefs)? How would you develop a relationship of trust?

3 Inviting a person to talk

One day Sarah, who works in our office, seemed to be very distracted and unable to concentrate. Kathryn noticed that Sarah was unable to focus on tasks that she needed to complete with some urgency, and her normal friendly manner had been replaced by rather brief, grumpy responses. Also, she looked as though she had slept in the clothes she was wearing and had forgotten to brush her hair, which she usually kept neat and tidy.

Kathryn had a number of alternatives:

1. She could have ignored Sarah's mood altogether and focused on her own work.
2. She could have talked to Sarah about the work she needed to do.
3. She could have said in a cheerful voice, 'You seem to be in a bit of a muddle today'.
4. She could have used some counselling skills to help Sarah explore her feelings and talk about what might be troubling her.

What would you have done in that situation? Our guess is that your decision about which alternative to use would have depended on a number of factors including your relationship with Sarah, the presence of other people, and work pressures. We have to recognise that often when people are working under high pressure there is little time available for listening to other people. There is a paradox here, however, because if we do take the time to listen to our colleagues so that they can deal with troubling issues, then often their ability to work happily and productively will improve.

It might be interesting to think about the various outcomes that could have occurred if Kathryn had used any of the alternatives listed.

If Kathryn had ignored Sarah's mood altogether it is possible that in time Sarah might have started to feel better and work more effectively. Unfortunately, it is equally possible that with time her mood might have stayed as it was or even have deteriorated.

If Kathryn had talked to Sarah about the work she needed to do, she would have probably have felt pressured because Kathryn is her supervisor. Sarah might also have felt resentful, believing that no one cared about her. Of course, it is possible that she might have made an effort and focused more effectively on her work.

Kathryn's third alternative, to say, 'You seem to be in a bit of a muddle today', involves using the counselling skill of giving feedback, as Kathryn would be feeding back to Sarah what she noticed. However, at this point in the process such an approach might not have been of very much use. This low-key approach might have helped Sarah to recognise the issues that were troubling her, but it is unlikely that she would have talked about them without further encouragement. It is more likely that she would have laughed weakly, deflected away from the issues that were troubling her, and replied by saying something like, 'Yes, I had a late night last night'. On the plus side she might have put more effort into trying to apply herself to her work. Unfortunately though, Sarah would have continued to be troubled by her problems and these would have been likely to continue to affect her work.

If Kathryn had decided to use some more relevant counselling skills it is quite probable that Sarah would have been able to deal with the things that were troubling her in a way that would have enabled her to put them to one side so that she could focus on her work.

NOTICING THAT HELP MAY BE NEEDED

Have you noticed what happens to your body, facial expression and general appearance when you are troubled by feelings and thoughts that are disturbing? Do you look the same as you do when nothing is worrying you? Is your behaviour the same or is it different?

We have noticed that when things are worrying us our facial expressions generally change and show that we are not feeling happy. We may even adopt a different posture so that other people might notice. Additionally, what we do, and the way we do things, will be affected. In particular, we are likely to find it harder to concentrate and apply ourselves effectively to tasks.

If we want to be helpful to people who are troubled we need to be very observant. It is only by being observant that you will be able to recognise someone else's discomfort.

NOTICING HOW OTHER PEOPLE LOOK, SPEAK, AND BEHAVE

If you get into the habit of casually and non-intrusively watching other people you will start to recognise the way we human beings inadvertently tell other people how we are feeling by the way that we present ourselves, talk and behave. When someone is emotionally uncomfortable they will either deliberately or unintentionally give out clues that something is wrong. You can use these clues to help you decide whether or not to use counselling skills. Sometimes the clues will be subtle and difficult to detect, so you may be uncertain about their meaning.

You might notice that a person is behaving in a way that is out of character and inconsistent with their normal behaviour. In particular, we suggest that you might want to look for any of the following:

- Someone who is normally bright, fun loving and energetic has become quiet, withdrawn and uncommunicative.
- A person who was previously cooperative appears to be deliberately uncooperative and unhelpful.
- The content or subject matter of a person's conversation continually seems to be focused around specific issues (for example, lack of money, illness or loneliness).
- A person who normally relates in a friendly way has withdrawn and seems to be keeping to themselves, not talking to anybody and to be brooding in silence.

- Someone who had previously taken a lot of care about their appearance now looks dishevelled and untidy.
- A person has 'bags' under their eyes as though they have been crying.
- Someone's facial expression suggests that they are very unhappy, unwell or anxious.
- Someone you know well is relating in a distant and hostile way to some members of their family or social network.
- Someone is unable to look at you directly.
- Someone is easily moved to tears.
- A person's tone of voice is depressed, or their voice quivers or falters.
- Someone is behaving in a way where they appear to be trying to look as though everything is okay, but where you sense that something is wrong. You might suspect that they are putting on a mask to cover up something which is going on underneath.

All of the above observations might suggest that a person could be experiencing painful emotions or be troubled by problems which require decisions. Can you add to this list?

To notice when other people are emotionally distressed observe:

- the way they look
- what they say
- how they speak
- how they move
- what they do

Once you have observed clues that suggest the possibility of emotional distress, you will have to make a decision: should you take action or not? You will need to decide whether or not to give the person concerned an invitation to talk to you. That is, you will need to decide whether or not to use counselling skills to invite the person to talk to you about their troubles.

INVITING THE PERSON TO TALK

Let's go back to the example involving Sarah that we described earlier. You might like to pause for a moment to think about what you might have said to Sarah if you had wanted to invite her to talk about her problems. We suggest that you think about this before reading on; because we are all different as individuals so we need to use counselling skills in a way that suits our individual personalities and ways of relating. Remember, every person brings into their relationships their own unique personality and style of relating. Consequently, when we make suggestions with regard to the use of suitable responses, it is important for you to modify these so that they suit you and your own individual style.

The first step in inviting a person to talk is to tell them what you have noticed about them or their behaviour. This is usually referred to as 'giving feedback'. The best way to give feedback is to be as specific and concrete as possible without being interpretive. For example, David might have given Sarah the following feedback:

I have noticed that several times you have stopped doing one job and started another.

This statement is more specific than saying, 'You seem to be easily distracted this morning'. Because it is more specific in directly drawing attention to the observed behaviour without interpretation, it is less likely to be challenged and more likely to be accepted. In contrast to this, the statement, 'You seem to be easily distracted this morning', might be incorrect. Sarah might not have been distracted, she might have been deliberately making decisions to change the tasks that she was doing before completing them.

Sometimes it is difficult, if not impossible, to be specific and concrete. In such a case, Kathryn might have used a more general statement in giving feedback to Sarah. She might have said something like:

Sarah, I've noticed that things seem to be getting the better of you today.

Sarah you don't seem to be your usual self today.

51

Unfortunately, feedback given on its own in this way may be seen as a criticism rather than an invitation to talk. So usually what we need to do is to follow up the feedback statement with a friendly, broadly framed, open question such as the following:

I am wondering if you've got something on your mind?

I am wondering whether or not something is troubling you?

Is something worrying you or are you okay?

If we combine these questions with the feedback statements we used before, typical invitations to talk are:

I have noticed that several times you have stopped doing one job and started another. I'm wondering if you've got something on your mind?

Sarah, I've noticed that things seem to be getting the better of you today. I am wondering whether or not something is troubling you?

Sarah you don't seem to be your usual self today. Is something worrying you or are you okay?

These initial invitations to talk each have the same format. They have two important characteristics:

1. They feed back to the person an accurate statement of what has been observed.
2. They ask a question about whether or not something is troubling or concerning the person. This question gives an indirect rather than a direct invitation to talk. It checks out whether the person concerned is troubled in some way.

Consider again the three invitations to talk that we have suggested Kathryn might have used with Sarah. In all three suggestions the invitation to Sarah would have been indirect and she would not have been asked directly whether she wanted to talk about troubling issues. Because the questions were indirect, Sarah was given the option of responding by saying something like, 'No, nothing's troubling me. I'm fine.' As a consequence Sarah would be unlikely to feel threatened by being trapped into disclosing personal information if she didn't want to. Sarah did however have an initial invitation to talk, and could have responded by saying something like, 'Actually, I am worried because ...', and have gone on to talk about her anxieties.

Notice also that the invitations suggested were general and not specific. For example, if Kathryn knew that Sarah had been having problems with her partner, Paul, she could have said, 'Sarah, I notice that you seem to be troubled today and I'm wondering whether this is because you're having problems with Paul?'. Using this question might have limited Sarah's reply to issues relating to her boyfriend. However, by using one of the more general open invitations as suggested earlier, Sarah would have been more likely to respond in an open way about the things which might have been troubling her. For example, she might not have been troubled by her boyfriend but might have been worrying because her mother had been admitted to hospital.

When you give a person an invitation to talk, it's important that the invitation is open, so that the person can talk about anything that troubles them rather than being limited to some specific topic which you have suggested.

> Initial invitations to talk need to consist of:
>
> • a feedback statement
> • a question which checks out whether or not the person is troubled

As stated earlier, the suggested invitations to Sarah were indirect. They did not include the question, 'Would you like to talk about your problem?'. All they did was to *enquire* about whether Sarah had a problem or not. Thus Sarah could easily have responded by starting to talk about a problem or by rejecting the implied invitation to talk and saying that everything was okay. If she did say that everything was okay, then it would have been important for Kathryn to have respected her response rather than to continue. However, if she responded positively to the initial invitation, then Kathryn would need to decide whether to build on that invitation, or not.

Sometimes an initial invitation to listen may be declined at the time when it is offered. However, if your reaction to the 'rejection' of your offer is positive, supportive and accepting, the person may feel able to approach you to talk about their problems at a later time.

Practice examples

You might like to take a few minutes to write down suggested invitations to talk that you might use in the situations described below:

1. *Imagine that you are a line manager*
   One of the people who works under your supervision has been in conflict with some of his workmates during the past few days and looks unhappy. You are concerned because he is normally easygoing, has good relationships with everyone, and seems to enjoy being at work. What would you say to give him an invitation to talk?

   . . . .

   . . . .

2. *Imagine that you are at a picnic with some close friends*
   You notice that one of your friends, Paula, who is normally very talkative, lively and vivacious, is avoiding talking to anyone in the group, including yourself, by engaging in unnecessary tasks which take her away from joining the group. What would you say to invite her to talk?

   . . . .

   . . . .

3. *Imagine that you are a nurse in a hospital*
   You have noticed that your patient, Mrs Brown, is always visibly upset after visits from her daughter Mary, but not after visits from other members of the family. What would you say to Mrs Brown to invite her to talk?

Now that you have completed these practice examples you might like to check to see whether your answers included the two important characteristics mentioned earlier in this chapter under Inviting the Person to Talk.

SHOULD THE INITIAL INVITATION TO TALK BE EXTENDED?

Figure 3.1 shows a flow chart illustrating the way in which the invitation for a person to talk can be extended. Starting from the top of the figure, you might notice how it relates to the example of Sarah. Initially her behaviour was noticed and then she was given the initial invitation to talk. Imagine that in responding to the initial invitation Sarah were to say, 'Actually I'm worried about my relationship with my mother'. At this point Kathryn would need to be aware that Sarah had not yet given her an indication that she wanted to continue talking about her problem. She had simply acknowledged and confirmed that Kathryn's observations and assumptions were correct and that she did have a problem. Although she had told Kathryn that the problem related to her mother she might not have wanted to give her any further information. Once again Kathryn would have a decision to make: should she give Sarah another invitation to continue or should she allow the conversation to end by saying something like, 'I'm sorry to hear that', and then change the subject or move away physically? This decision would depend on Kathryn's personal judgement but would need to take into account:

1. The appropriateness of the situation.
2. The timing.
3. Whether Kathryn was the right person or not.

Consider the influence of these factors when making a decision to give a further invitation to a person to continue talking.

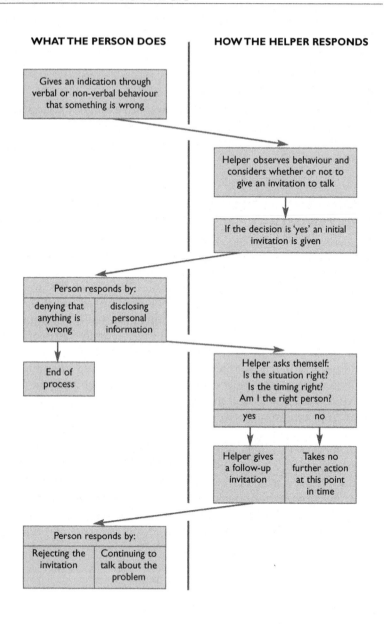

Figure 3.1 Inviting a person to talk about their worries

Is the situation right?

We need to be very careful when we invite people to talk to us to ensure that we don't create an embarrassing situation for them. If there are other people around who might hear what is being said it might be difficult and/or embarrassing for a person to disclose anything of a personal nature. Additionally, if the issues are painful, when the person starts to talk about them they might become even more distressed and start to cry. In a work situation this is likely to be embarrassing. This can also be true in many other situations such as social, community, educational, medical and religious settings, because most people don't like other people to see them crying.

Have you noticed how most people prefer to give others the impression that they are fine? Often, when you ask someone, 'How are you today?' the response is usually, 'Fine' or, 'Very well thank you', even though that may not always be true. There are a number of reasons why people tend to respond this way. Major reasons are that most people like to keep their problems to themselves to preserve their privacy and most people find it embarrassing when other people see them behaving emotionally. Additionally, many people rightly believe that other people will not want to listen to their problems. Interestingly, one day when David rang a pizza delivery service the operator began by asking him, 'How are you today'. When he mischievously replied, 'Actually I am quite sick', and went on to tell the operator about his problems, it was clear that the person he was talking to was at a loss to know what to do and certainly did not want to hear about his problems. Naturally, David realised that what he had done in jest was inappropriate and apologised. Isn't it interesting that socially many people ask, 'How are you today?', but only want to hear the answer if it is a positive one. It is important to recognise that when making a decision to extend the invitation to talk, you are sincerely and intentionally offering the other person an opportunity to talk about how they feel and to elaborate on their problem.

When considering privacy, the appropriateness of the physical environment is of major importance. It may be, for example, that Sarah would not want to disclose personal issues in the work environment. However, she might be quite happy to do this in the coffee shop around the corner. Consequently, when we try to help someone we need to be aware of that person's needs in this regard and be able to make suggestions which will allow them to recognise that talking in the present context may not be sensible.

Is the timing right?

Sometimes, although the situation may be suitable, the timing will not be appropriate. Imagine that Sarah had a large amount of work that urgently needed to be completed. In this case it would probably have been inappropriate for someone to encourage Sarah to start talking about her personal problems. To do so would just have increased Sarah's anxiety. However, having said this, we have to point out that sometimes the opposite can be true (there is an exception to every rule!). It might have been that Sarah was so overwhelmed by her emotions that she was unable to focus on her work. In such a case it would have been appropriate to invite Sarah to talk so that she could at least ventilate some of her feelings.

Clearly, deciding when to ask someone to talk about their problems is a very subjective process where we need to be sensitive to, and respectful of, the person we would like to help, and to make judgements which are likely to suit the person concerned and are appropriate for the situation.

Are you the right person?

Before inviting someone to talk to you, you need to consider the question, 'Am I the right person, or not?'. We believe that it is important for all of us to maintain consistent relationships with other people, because if we don't, our relationships are certain to be impaired by diminished levels of trust. We need to recognise that when we invite someone to talk with us about their personal problems, the relationship we have with them may change in some way. Therefore, before we invite someone to talk with us we need to decide whether or not it is appropriate for us to do so.

Before we invite someone to talk with us we need to take into account issues raised in Chapter 2 with regard to differences, including gender, culture and race. We need to think about our own and the other person's need to set appropriate boundaries relevant for the situation. We must consider the need for privacy and confidentiality and ask ourselves whether these can be met within the context of our relationship with the person. In a work environment we need to consider whether there will be a conflict between our obligations to our employer or agency and our need to respect the other person's privacy. If we are in a position of authority, we need to recognise that the other person may feel intimidated or intruded upon if we are not careful to be sensitive and tentative in our invitations.

We always need to consider the possibility that if a person talks to us about private information this is likely to have an effect of some kind on our relationship with them. There may also be impli-cations regarding our relationships with the person's colleagues, relatives or friends.

Above all, before inviting a person to talk we need to think about whether the relationship we have with them is sufficiently trusting for them to be able to usefully talk with us.

> Before inviting a person to continue talking we need to ask:
> - Is the situation right?
> - Is the timing right?
> - Am I the right person?

You may decide from the person's initial response that you are not the best person for them to talk to about their worries. At this point what do you think that you might say and do? We think that you will probably agree with us in believing that acknowledging the current difficulties the person is experiencing by making a respectful and caring response is appropriate. For example, in the situation with Sarah, if Kathryn had thought that she was not the right person she might have said, 'I'm sorry to hear that you're having problems with your mother; that must be worrying for you'. This would let Sarah know that she had been heard and understood without expecting her to disclose more information. Additionally, Kathryn might raise the possibility that Sarah may want to talk to someone else about her worries. This would give Sarah a clear message that Kathryn was not offering to help Sarah herself.

OFFERING A FURTHER INVITATION

If in your opinion the timing is right, the situation is right, and you have a suitable relationship with the person concerned, you may decide to extend the invitation for them to talk to you about their problems. Figure 3.1 illustrates the process involved in inviting a person to talk.

Extending the invitation invites the person to *continue* talking about the problem in more detail. Consider the example of Sarah. Imagine that Sarah responds to the initial invitation by saying, 'I'm worried about my relationship with my mother'. Pause for a moment and think about how you could extend the invitation further so that Sarah would feel welcome to continue talking to you about her problem if she wants to, but free to keep her problems to herself, if that is what she prefers.

Would it have been appropriate for Kathryn to say to Sarah, 'What's the problem with your relationship with your mother?' or, 'Can you tell me what's happened in your relationship with your mother?'.

Although those invitations could have been used, we wouldn't recommend them because they are very direct and might have been intrusive. It might be that Sarah didn't want to talk to Kathryn about her problem in more detail. It may have been sufficient for Sarah to just let Kathryn know that she had a problem.

We prefer to couch invitations to continue talking in such a way that the other person will find it easy to accept the invitation if they want to, or to reject it without feeling bad about doing so. Consequently, we might say something like:

> *I'm sorry to hear that your relationship with your mother is worrying you, and I'm wondering whether you would like to talk to me about it or not?*

or,

> *I'm sorry to hear that. Do you think that talking to me about it might help, or would that be something you'd rather not do?*

or,

> *Sarah, I'm sorry to hear that. I sometimes worry too when things are bothering me and I find that it helps if I talk to someone. I'm wondering if you would like to talk to me about what's happening, or whether that would be too difficult for you, in this situation?*

or,

> *Sarah, it sounds as though things are difficult for you. I know that right now might not be a good opportunity for you to talk, and you might not even want to do that, but I'd like you to know that if you would like to talk to me either now or later, that would be okay for me.*

What do you notice about the invitations suggested above? They all have the following characteristics:

1. They start with an acknowledgment of the person's feelings, and/or problem.
2. They are framed in a way that invites the person to continue talking or to reject the offer.

Notice that if you are to help other people talk freely with you, you will need to give them clear invitations to talk in a way which allows them to choose to do this, or to feel okay about not accepting your offer. By framing your invitation appropriately, the person will know that it is genuine and that they are being offered a definite opportunity to talk.

> Follow-up invitations to talk:
>
> • Acknowledge the person's feelings and/or problem
> • Invite the person to continue talking or to comfortably reject the invitation

Follow-up practice examples

You might like to go back to the practice examples used earlier to see whether you can think of suitable ways to invite the person to continue talking. Remember that what you say should start by acknowledging the other person's feelings and/or problem, and should then give an invitation to the person to continue talking or allow them to reject your offer with ease.

1. *Imagine that you are a line manager*
   Also imagine that the person to whom you gave the initial invitation to talk has responded by saying, 'Yes, everybody has been picking on me lately'. How would you give them an invitation to continue talking about their problem?

   . . . .

   . . . .

2. *Imagine that you are at a picnic with some close friends*
   Also imagine that after giving Paula the initial invitation to talk, Paula responds by saying, 'Oh it's nothing really, I'm just having trouble trying to make a decision'. What could you say to invite her to continue talking?

   . . . .

   . . . .

3. *Imagine that you are a nurse in a hospital*
   Also imagine that Mrs Brown has responded to your initial invitation by saying, 'I just seem to get stressed every time she visits'. What would you say to invite her to continue talking?

   . . . .

   . . . .

THE INVITATION TO TALK IS ACCEPTED

We have now reached the point in Figure 3.1 where the person may have accepted your invitation and may continue to talk about their problems. As this happens, try to build and maintain a relationship which values the person as explained in Chapter 2. If you do, the skills described in the following chapters have the best chance of being effective in helping the person.

BEING APPROACHED FOR HELP

As discussed in Chapter 1, some people have a high level of natural listening and helping skills with the result that other people will often approach them to talk about their problems. Once you have learnt and become competent in using some basic counselling skills, you may find that people will, at times, approach you for help because they recognise that you are a good listener. Sometimes these approaches may be direct and a friend, colleague or client may ask you, 'Is it okay if I talk to you about this problem that I have?'. Alternatively, they may start talking to you about the problem without even asking you whether it is okay to do so. At other times someone may approach you in a tentative and indirect way. Although you may have a reputation for being a good listener, some people may not feel confident about approaching you directly for assistance. In these situations, the observational and inviting skills that we have discussed earlier can be useful.

ARRANGING A TIME TO TALK

Sometimes a person may want to talk to you about personal matters at a time, and in a situation, which is unsuitable or inconvenient for you. For example, you may be in the middle of completing an important task; you may have to rush off to a meeting; or you may be feeling too pressured to be able to listen. Even so, you may think that it is appropriate and sensible for the person to be given the opportunity to talk with you at a different time and/or a different place. It is then sensible to make it clear that right now is neither suitable nor convenient and suggest an alternative time and place when and where you will feel less pressured by your commitments, in a better position to listen, and where there may be a higher level of privacy. You might offer an invitation to meet at another time by saying:

> *Unfortunately right now is not a good time for me. Would you like to meet in either my office or your office later today? In this way we will have more privacy, and can talk more freely. What time would be good for you?*

By giving such an invitation, an arrangement can be made so that a longer confidential discussion, free from interruption, is possible. In such a setting it is important to be clear about expectations and about the nature of the relationship. Always remember that appropriate ethical boundaries must be respected as explained in Chapter 2.

REFERRAL TO QUALIFIED HELPERS

As you continue to listen to a person's story, it may be that you will realise that the person's problems are such that help from a suitably qualified counsellor or other professional is required. In this case, in order to satisfy the ethical demands of the situation, we strongly suggest that you should talk to the person directly and openly about your concern for them and let them know that you believe that it would be sensible for them to talk to someone who has the required qualifications and expertise to help them. By doing this you are being responsible and are likely to be trusted and respected because you are able to recognise your limitations and ensure that the person gets the most appropriate help.

You might find it useful to find out about counselling, mental health and other resources available in your area or your place of work. Also you might want to find out the processes required to enable people to access those services. By doing this, when you recognise that someone needs qualified help you will be in a position to be able to make sensible suggestions.

WHEN YOUR INVITATION IS REFUSED

It may be that you will give an invitation to talk to someone who is uncomfortable about sharing personal information with you. This is certain to happen at times, so we hope that you will not see this as personal rejection when it does. Most people are very selective about who they feel able to confide in. This issue is particularly relevant in work situations. However, provided that your reaction to someone who declines your invitation to talk with you is positive, supportive and accepting, then that person may possibly feel comfortable enough to approach you at a later time to talk about their problems.

When someone makes it clear that they have worries but can't share them with you, you may wish to raise the possibility that they might be helped by talking with someone else. In this case, if it is true, you might say:

John, from time to time I've had a number of personal problems myself and I've found it useful to talk to someone I trust about those problems. Sometimes I've talked to a friend and when the problems that were troubling me were very personal I have talked to a counsellor. I wonder if you would find it useful to talk to a friend or a counsellor about the things that are troubling you?

If the response is positive, then, if you know of a suitable counsellor, you might want to continue by saying:

I can recommend somebody you could talk to confidentially away from this setting.

Sometimes you may invite a person to talk to you and discover that they are already talking with a counsellor. In this case it's important to respect this and not actively encourage the person to talk to you as well, as you may inadvertently compromise the work that the counsellor is doing.

POSSIBLE RESPONSES TO PRACTICE EXAMPLES

1. The line manager

Initial invitation: 'Frank, you usually get on very well with everyone at work, but I've noticed that in the last day or two you seem to be having some difficulty getting on with the others. I'm wondering if something is bothering you?'

Further invitation: 'I'm sorry to hear that. Would it help for you to talk to me about what's happening or would you rather sort things out yourself?'

2. **The friend**

   Initial invitation: 'You are very quiet today Paula. Is everything OK?'

   Further invitation: 'Making decisions can be hard. Can I be of help, or is it better for you to figure things out yourself?'

3. **The nurse**

   Initial invitation: 'You seemed to enjoy having your family to visit, but I've noticed that you appear to get upset when Mary visits. Does something trouble you when Mary visits?'

   Further invitation: 'That must be hard for you especially when you're not well. Would you like to talk some more about how you feel or would you rather keep things to yourself?'

chapter summary

- The first steps in offering to help are to observe and to give the person needing help an invitation to talk.

- Notice when a person needs help by observing the way they look, what they say and do, and their non-verbal behaviour.

- The initial invitation to talk involves feeding back to the person what has been observed, and using an open question to give the person an indirect invitation to talk which can easily be accepted or rejected.

- We need to be sensitive with regard to whether the situation and timing are appropriate.

- The invitation to continue talking should start with an acknowledgement of the person's pain, and be framed in a way that allows the person to accept or reject the invitation.

- We all need to recognise our limits and refer to qualified and experienced helpers when necessary.

ASSIGNMENT EXERCISES FOR COURSEWORK STUDENTS

1. Consider each of the scenarios listed below. For each scenario suggest a response that you would use to give the person an initial invitation to talk. Then write down a brief description of a possible response from the person. Follow this by suggesting a second response that you would use to invite the person to continue talking.

   a. *Imagine that you are a human resources officer*
   A member of staff tells you how well she is doing in a new position, but while telling you this you notice that she seems to be both agitated and stressed. She is talking very quickly and seems to be getting out of breath.

   b. *Imagine that you are a person who delivers meals to elderly people in their homes*
   An elderly man who lives on his own and is usually quite friendly and chatty barely greets you. When you put his meal down in front of him he pushes it away.

   c. *Imagine that you are a doctor*
   You have just told a patient that their pathology tests showed no abnormality. The patient responds by looking troubled and dismayed.

2. Think of a real situation in your life where you would recognise that it would not be appropriate for you to invite another person to share problems at the time when they were meeting with you. Describe the situation, what you think your own feelings would be and how these would impact on you, what you would do or say, and whether you would take any subsequent action or not. Briefly discuss what would influence your decision.

4 Skills to help the person continue talking

It doesn't matter who you are, whether you are a manager, a medical practitioner, a religious leader, a workmate, a neighbour or a friend, if you want to be helpful to someone who is troubled or has a worrying problem, the most important thing you can do is listen to them. You need to listen to them in a way which helps them to feel comfortable about sharing information with you. This is not always as easy as it sounds because many people who have a problem find it difficult to talk to other people about things that might be emotionally troubling for them. It follows that if you are to be helpful in listening to other people you will need to learn some particular skills which are useful in encouraging them to continue talking freely and openly to you.

You might like to take a few moments to think about what it's like for yourself. When something is troubling you, who are you most likely to confide in? Is it someone who gives you advice, or is it someone who listens to what you have to say? We think, provided that you have established a relationship of the type described in Chapter 2, that the next most important quality required, if you are to help someone, is the ability to use skills which will invite and enable the other person to talk while you listen.

> The person being helped needs to feel valued

As discussed previously, the person being helped needs to feel valued, regardless of anything they may have done. If we want to bring out the best in people, we have to recognise their worth and value them regardless of their behaviour. Paradoxically, the best way to help a person to change unacceptable behaviour is to accept them as they are.

ACTIVE LISTENING

The best way to help a person feel valued is by actively listening in a focused and attentive way as they talk about their problems. By showing that you are serious in your concern for them, and interested in listening to them, you will inevitably encourage them to continue talking so that they can explore their problems fully.

There are two important ways of encouraging a person to continue talking to you while letting them know that you are actively listening in a caring and focused way. These are:

1. To join with the person by letting them know that you are listening.
2. To let the person know that you have heard and understand what they are saying.

JOINING BY LETTING THE PERSON KNOW THAT YOU ARE LISTENING

Have you ever talked about being on the same 'wavelength' as someone? Maybe you have sometimes noticed that a person has really 'tuned in' to what you are saying. Joining is about 'tuning in', or 'being on the same wavelength' as someone else. Thus, a harmonious connection is established between the person who is talking and the person who is listening. This is what we need to achieve if we are to encourage a person to talk openly with us.

Whenever we listen to someone, we give out very subtle clues. These clues give an indication of how we are responding to what is being said, and of our feelings towards the person who is speaking. We therefore need to be careful to give out the right messages.

> When we listen we give out subtle messages

Imagine that you were talking to someone about a problem of yours which was difficult or embarrassing for you to talk about. While you were talking, you might wonder what the person

69

concerned was thinking about you, and about what you were saying. Unless the listener gave you some reassuring clues, you could start thinking negative thoughts like these:

1. This person is disgusted by or disapproves of what I am saying.
2. This person really doesn't want to hear what I am saying.
3. This person is only listening to me out of politeness.
4. This person is in a hurry to get away.
5. I'm making this person feel uncomfortable.
6. This person doesn't respect me.

People who are troubled by things that worry them are often embarrassed or ashamed of some of the things they have to say. They are therefore likely to jump to negative conclusions unless you are able to give clear messages about your attitude to them and to what they are saying. If you want the person to continue talking you will need to give out positive messages which say something like, 'I respect you as a person; what you are saying is important to me, and I feel valued to know that you are trusting me with this information'.

What do you think you can do, or say, to convey the appropriate message? You could, of course, use the direct approach and say something like:

> *I believe that what you are saying is important. Would you like to tell me more?*

A statement like this would be helpful, but to be convincing it would have to be accompanied by a number of other helpful behaviours, which we will describe under the following headings:

- Eye contact
- Facial expression
- Physical closeness
- Body posture
- Voice matching
- Short responses
- Non-verbal responses.

Eye contact

How often have you heard a parent say to a child, 'look at me when I'm talking to you'? We think that it is quite common for parents to say this, because when you talk to someone and they don't look at you, you are likely to get the impression that they are not listening. It follows that if we are to join with someone we need to make appropriate eye contact with them. By doing this, they are likely to realise that we are paying attention to what they are saying. When making eye contact we need to be sensitive to what is appropriate for the person we are making contact with, as there are cultural differences with regard to levels of eye contact.

Regardless of culture, it would clearly not be appropriate to continually stare into someone else's eyes while they were talking. This would make them feel uncomfortable. However, equally it would not be appropriate to spend most of the time looking away, because they would believe that we weren't listening. Obviously, there needs to be a sensible balance so that we consistently make eye contact, while glancing away at times.

When we are trying to help someone we need to remember that we can give subtle messages of approval or disapproval with our eyes. Similarly we can convey feelings of amusement, or use our eyes to convey the message that we are serious in paying attention and listening to what is being said.

Facial expression

We talk about some people having 'poker' faces because we find it difficult to tell what they are thinking by looking at their facial expression. If you were talking to someone like that, you would be likely to feel uncomfortable and wonder what was going on in their mind. If we are trying to help someone, we need to join with them. They need to believe that we are attending to what they say in a respectful away. They need to get a message which suggests that we are interested in what they are saying, and most importantly that we do not disapprove of or judge them. In order to do this we need to remember the importance of our facial expression.

71

Physical closeness

Have you noticed what happens to you when someone stands too close to you for your own comfort? Also, have you noticed how you feel when you are talking to someone and they move away from you or stand a long way away from you. We all have our own comfort level with regard to physical closeness, and of course this will vary depending on the relationship we have with the person who is talking to us. Clearly, physical closeness conveys a message. If we stand too far away, the person we are listening to may well feel as though we are not interested in what they are saying. If we stand too close to them they may feel as though their personal boundaries are being invaded and may want to withdraw. When considering physical closeness we need to recognise that there are particular difficulties when we are talking with someone from a different culture, as what is normal in one culture may be different from what is normal in another. We can't always know what is right in terms of physical closeness. However, if we are sensitive to the responses of the other person we can usually adjust the distance between us so that they feel more comfortable and believe that we want to join with them in an appropriate way.

Body posture

The position and posture of your body will give significant messages to the person who has come for help. Generally, the best approach is to try to adopt a similar posture to that of the person who is talking to you. If they are standing up straight, then they will probably feel most comfortable if you do the same. If they are sitting in a relaxed position then they will probably feel most comfortable if you model your own physical behaviour on theirs. This is called, 'matching'. Quite clearly, if you were to over-exaggerate matching and behave as though you were a mirror image of the person, they might wonder whether you were trying to mimic them and be embarrassed. However, a sensible level of matching enables the person to feel comfortable with you without noticing what you are doing.

Voice matching

Another type of matching relates to tone of voice, loudness or softness of speaking and rate of speaking. Sometimes the person who is talking to you will be agitated and will speak hurriedly and quickly. Initially, it may be useful for you to match this hurried style as a way of joining.

One of the advantages of matching is that it tends to become reciprocal. For example, if you have matched the speed of talking with someone who is agitated and then you start to slow down your own speech, it's probable that the other person will also slow down their speech. In this way it's possible to help an agitated person to slow down and become calm. Once again, matching needs to be done sensibly or the person may feel as though you are mimicking them.

Short responses

Imagine that you are listening on the telephone. How do you let the caller know that you are still there without interrupting what they are saying? What most people do is to use short responses such as:

Ah ha, Mmmm, Yes, Really, Oh, Right,

or slightly longer responses such as:

Is that so?, I see, or *I understand.*

These responses are not intrusive, but are an indication to the caller that you are listening. They are needed in face-to-face situations, as well as on the phone.

A word of warning: if short verbal responses are used too frequently they become intrusive. If they are not used frequently enough then the person you are helping may not feel encouraged to continue talking, and may feel that you are not interested in what they are saying. Clearly, we need to use our personal judgement in this matter.

Non-verbal responses

We can also make it clear that we are interested and are listening by using non-verbal responses such as a nod or shake of the head, or a facial expression.

> Effective helpers actively listen and leave most of the talking to the other person

We have now discussed a range of useful behaviours which help the person who is talking to recognise that you value them and are listening to them.

As we have discussed previously, a helping conversation is different from most other social or professional conversations. Most everyday conversations move backwards and forwards equally between the talkers. However, when you are trying to help someone who is troubled by a personal, emotional or relationship problem, most of the talking should be done by the person who is being helped. This is very different from conversations generally, because we have all learnt to behave socially by taking turns when talking with someone else. In most conversations we will introduce our own ideas as frequently as other people. Because of this, helping behaviour seems to be unnatural at first because it involves a lot of listening and not so much talking.

When you are trying to help someone else deal with a problem try to avoid focusing on what you need to say. Instead, focus on what the other person is telling you. If, particularly in the initial stages of the conversation, you listen quietly, give short verbal and non-verbal responses, and only speak when you need to say something useful, the other person is likely to feel heard and valued. However, as the conversation progresses, if you were to listen and just use short responses, and say little else, then the person being helped might become disillusioned and believe that you weren't really interested in their problems. Clearly, if you are to be helpful, the conversation needs to be an *active listening* process rather than just a passive listening process.

LETTING THE PERSON KNOW THAT YOU HAVE HEARD AND UNDERSTOOD

As we have discussed, in the early stages of a conversation where you are trying to help someone the emphasis is on listening, but not just in a passive way. You need to let the person being helped know that you have not only listened but that you have also *heard and understood*. The best way to do this is through the use of the skill called 'reflection'.

Reflection of feelings and content

Reflection relies heavily on listening intently to what is being said and noticing how the person is saying it. Imagine that someone says to you, 'I'm going to be in trouble with my boss if I take another day off work sick'. When you hear this, you might recognise two things:

1. That the person is worried.
2. That the problem is related to the boss's response, if the person takes another day off work sick.

Do you notice the difference between 1 and 2 above? The first thing recognised, that the person is worried, concerns the person's *emotional feelings*. The second thing recognised, that the problem is related to taking another day off work, involves the *content* of the message.

When reflecting, it is important to recognise the difference between *emotional feelings* and *content*. You can then learn how to reflect both of these either separately or together, depending on which is most appropriate.

What is reflection?

When you look in a mirror you see your own reflection, and this gives you important information about yourself. When you are

75

trying to help someone and you use reflection, you act rather like a mirror. What you do is to reflect back to the person, not how they look, but what they are saying and/or feeling.

In the example given, you could reflect back the emotional feeling of being worried by saying:

You're worried

or you could reflect back the content of what the person was saying, by responding with:

Taking another day off work might create some difficulties for you.

Do you notice the difference between reflection of feelings and reflection of content as exemplified by the responses above? In one case the underlying emotional feeling of worry was reflected back, and in the other case the content of what had been said, that is, the concrete facts of the situation, were reflected back. Alternatively, both the emotional feeling and the content could have been reflected back by saying:

You are worried about the consequences of taking another day off work.

Notice that in each of the examples given above, reflection by the helper didn't repeat word for word what the person said, but expressed things differently. Thus, the helper used their own words rather than the other person's. This is essential, otherwise the person being helped might not believe that they were being understood, and might think that the helper was behaving like a parrot!

> When reflecting use your own words

Consider another example where reflection could be used. Imagine that a person says to you, 'My son hasn't rung me for such a long time. I thought he would, because I sent a birthday present to him last week.' Suitable helping reflections might be:

You sound disappointed. (reflection of emotional feeling)

You expected to hear from your son. (reflection of content)

You sound disappointed because you haven't heard from your son. (reflection of feeling and content)

It might be interesting for you to notice that generally reflection of feelings involves 'feeling' words which are single words. We have found that quite often people confuse reflection of feelings and reflection of content and do not recognise the importance of the difference. If you say, for example, 'I feel as though it's going to rain today', you have expressed a thought rather than an emotional feeling, and it would probably have been more accurate to have said, 'I think it's going to rain today'.

If you were to say, 'I feel frightened', then you would be reflecting an emotional feeling. Notice that 'frightened' is a single word. Compare this with the string of words, 'as though it's going to rain today', from the previous statement.

Below is a list of feeling words which could be used when you are reflecting feelings.

Words to express emotional feelings

sad	happy	angry	disappointed
confused	relaxed	worried	anxious
frustrated	concerned	puzzled	furious
disappointed	heartbroken	depressed	elated
excited	agitated	tired	lethargic
energetic	devastated	embarrassed	ecstatic
terrified	miserable	elated	pleased
resentful	guilty	energised	
ashamed	proud	mystified	

You might like to check through these and see whether or not you can think of any additional feeling words which could be included in this list.

Additional words:...

If you look at the words listed above you will notice that we can make sentences by just putting the words, 'You feel', in front of any of them. By doing this we create a sentence which can be used, in an appropriate situation, as a reflection of feeling.

In practice, we don't need to use the words 'you feel' at all when we reflect feelings. We can reflect feelings by saying things like, 'you're sad', 'you're frustrated', or 'you're delighted', without having the word 'feel' in the sentence.

Pausing before reflecting

Have you noticed that in general conversation people often interrupt each other? They do this because they are keen to say something themselves. Additionally, when they don't interrupt they will usually reply as soon as the other person has finished their sentence. This common conversational behaviour is not useful when we are trying to help someone. If we are trying to help someone we need to observe them as they talk to us. If we watch their eyes and facial expressions we will often be able to recognise that after saying something to us, they will continue thinking about what they have said. If we don't interrupt them they are able to continue to talk to us more fully about their thoughts. It is therefore important that, when we are listening to someone, we pause before reflecting back what they have said or what they are feeling. This pause allows them time to think, and time to continue what they are saying if they wish to do so. Initially many people find it uncomfortable to pause before responding because they are not used to doing this in general conversation. Additionally, during a pause there is a period of silence. Many people are uncomfortable with silence in general conversation and feel obliged to fill in any gaps. Even so, if you are to be a good helper you need to be able to give the person you're helping time to think and complete what they are saying before you interrupt.

> Take time – allow pauses – don't interrupt

What do we hope to achieve by using reflection?

Reflection achieves three things:

1. It allows the person to recognise that the helper is listening, has heard, and understands what they are saying.
2. It enables the person to get more fully in touch with their emotional feelings and with the content of what they are saying.
3. It encourages the person to continue talking.

You may be wondering why we've stressed the need to learn the difference between reflecting feelings and reflecting content. The reason is that sometimes it's more useful to *just* reflect feelings. When you just reflect a feeling without reflecting content, if the reflection is accurate, the other person will be able to get more fully in touch with, and express the relevant feeling. For example, if you reflect back the feeling of sadness by saying,

You're very sad

or

You sound sad when you tell me that

then the person who is talking to you may get more fully in touch with their sadness and start to cry. Often this will be useful in enabling them to let their sadness out rather than bottling it up. Clearly, if you reflect feelings you need to be prepared for the person's emotional response and this may be uncomfortable for you as they may express strong emotions. Additionally, you need to take account of the situation. In an environment where other people are present, it may be inappropriate and/or embarrassing for the person you are helping to express strong emotions. In such a situation it may be more useful to just reflect content so that the person can continue to tell you more of their story without getting more fully in touch with their emotional feelings.

It is often useful to reflect both content and feelings. Although this may help the person to get in touch with a strong emotion, it also offers them the opportunity to focus on the content of what they are saying, rather than their emotions, if that is what they prefer to do.

With practice and experience you will be able to recognise when it is most appropriate to reflect feelings, or to reflect content, or to reflect both content and feelings. There is no formula for making this decision. You will need to use your intuition and experience.

PRACTICE EXAMPLES

There follow some examples of statements which a troubled person might make. You might like to see whether for each example you can think of statements that you could use to do each of the following:

1. To reflect feelings
2. To reflect content
3. To reflect feelings and content.

At the end of this chapter, we have suggested responses which we ourselves might use.

In creating responses try to use different words from those used in the statement, and keep your responses as short as possible. You don't need to reflect the whole of a statement, just what you think is important.

The responses which you create will be different from the ones which we have suggested, because we are different people. When working on these examples, it is important to recognise that the person's statements can sometimes be interpreted in several different ways, particularly when they are in writing. When a person actually speaks to you, you may be able to detect sadness, happiness or frustration, just by listening to the person's tone of voice. Clearly you can't do this in the same way when reading what has been said.

Example 1

'My mother's quite an old lady and last night she phoned me to say that she'd had a fall. It seemed as though she'd cracked her knee on the stairs. I wish I didn't live so far away.'

Example 2

'My daughter is being really disobedient and is creating a lot of trouble. She is continually causing fights by starting arguments with her brother and my husband.'

Example 3

'This contract is very important to me. I sent a fax to the company last week and I've had no response. This is very strange because, up to now, they seemed to be very keen to try to reach agreement with me on the terms of the contract.'

Example 4

'My son is getting married in Birmingham. He is marrying a very nice person and I'm really looking forward to going to the wedding.'

Example 5

'My boss has some really good ideas. This particular project is sure to be a winner and it looks to me as though I'm going to get the credit because he has given me the task of coordinating the work.'

Example 6

'My lecturer has given me this assignment to do. I've looked everywhere for resources and information to help me but I can't find anything.'

IN CONCLUSION

When using reflection, don't worry excessively if your reflections are occasionally inaccurate. If you make an inaccurate reflection the person concerned is likely to correct your statement, and in doing so will think more clearly about how they feel about the situation.

We have been looking at ways in which we can join with a person and enable them to feel valued by listening in a manner which will let them know that their story is important to us. Once a person's story has started to unfold you may find that it is quite complicated and confusing for them. You will then need to help them sort through what they have told you so that the situation is less confusing for them. By doing this you will enable them to focus on the central or essential problem. Ways to do this will be discussed in the next chapter.

RESPONSES TO PRACTICE EXAMPLES

Here are our suggested responses to the practice examples given previously:

Example 1

'You sound worried' (reflection of feeling).

'You're worried' (reflection of feeling).

'Your mother may have hurt herself' (reflection of content).

'You're worried about your mother' (reflection of feeling and content).

'You sound worried about your mother because you think that she has hurt herself' (reflection of feeling and content).

or,

'You are concerned about your mother and wish you lived nearer to her' (reflection of feeling and content).

Example 2

'You sound angry' (reflection of feeling).

'You're angry' (reflection of feeling).

'Your daughter is causing a lot of trouble' (reflection of content).

'You're angry because your daughter is causing trouble' (reflection of feeling and content).

Example 3

'You're puzzled' (reflection of feeling).

'You're worried' (reflection of feeling).

'You seem to be puzzled and worried' (reflection of feelings, notice that two feelings have been reflected here).

'Although this company gave you the impression that they wanted to negotiate with you, now you're not getting responses' (reflection of content).

'You're puzzled and worried because you haven't had a response from this company' (reflection of feelings and content).

Example 4

'You sound happy' (reflection of feeling).

'I get the impression that you are very happy' (reflection of feeling).

'You're pleased' (reflection of feeling).

'You're going to your son's wedding in Birmingham' (reflection of content).

'You sound happy to be going to your son's wedding' (reflection of content and feeling).

Example 5

'You sound delighted' (reflection of feeling).

'So you're delighted' (reflection of feeling).

'Your boss has given you responsibility for a worthwhile project' (reflection of content).

'You sound delighted to have been given responsibility for the project' (reflection of content and feeling).

Example 6

'You sound frustrated' (reflection of feeling).

83

'You seem to be frustrated' (reflection of feeling).

'So, you're frustrated' (reflection of feeling).

'Even though you've looked, you can't find what you need' (reflection of content).

'You're frustrated at not being able to find the information you need (refection of content and feeling).

chapter summary

- To help others, the emphasis needs to be on listening rather than talking yourself.

- When joining and listening we need to take account of eye contact, facial expression, physical closeness, body posture, voice, pauses, and we need to use non-verbal and short verbal responses.

- Feelings are different from thoughts and can be expressed in single words.

- Reflection of feelings involves letting the person know that you have recognised how they are feeling emotionally.

- Reflection of content involves restating the most important part of what the person has shared, briefly and in your own words.

- Use of reflection:
  - Lets the person know that you are listening and understand.
  - Helps the person to get more fully in touch with emotional feelings.
  - Encourages the person to continue talking about the content of what they have been saying.

ASSIGNMENT EXERCISES FOR COURSEWORK STUDENTS

1. Think about a situation in your past where you have been able to talk freely with someone else about a personal problem. Describe the special characteristics of the situation, and the qualities and behaviours of the other person, which enabled you to feel welcome to talk about your problem. (There is no need for you to disclose the nature of the problem unless you wish to do so.)

2. Below is a list of statements made by people who have a problem which troubles them. For each statement provide a reflection of feelings, a reflection of content and a reflection of feelings and content.

   a. I think I'm going to lose my job and if I do it will be a disaster. I just don't know how I'll be able to afford the repayments on my mortgage.

   b. I am trying to concentrate at work, but my wife is dying of cancer. It's all overwhelming because she is so important to me and our children.

   c. My boss says that I've got to present a report at the meeting of senior management even though he knows I'm terrified of public speaking.

   d. I really need my car to get to the shops and do my shopping, but my son says that I'm too old to drive. I don't know what to do.

   e. I don't want to have those medical tests because I'm frightened that there might be something seriously wrong with me and I'd rather not know.

   f. I'm a total failure because I never seem to be able to complete any job that I start. I might as well give up altogether!

5 Helping the person to feel better

Imagine that someone comes to you with a problem that is troubling them. How are you going to help them to feel better? Perhaps you can think of a time when you had a problem and someone helped you to feel better. Can you remember what the other person did that helped? You might like to jot down one or two notes about what you remember:

....

....

....

We think that generally there is a process that needs to occur in order to help a troubled person move into a more comfortable space. Underlying and central to this process is a need for the person concerned to feel that the person who is offering help has joined with them and values them. The relationship which a helper develops with a troubled person is, in our opinion, the most important attribute of the helping process. It is the quality of the relationship which helps the person to feel valued without being judged. They are then able to move forward in a climate of acceptance.

Helping someone to feel better involves a process and not just a single event. The process starts when the person recognises that someone else cares enough to invite them to share their troubling thoughts and emotions. By using the skills described in the previous chapters, the helper can enable the troubled person to talk about their problem and share their thoughts and emotions. Thus the person is enabled to recognise, get in touch with, express and ventilate their emotional feelings. By doing this they are able to see more clearly the issues which are troubling them. They are then in a position where they may be able to focus on the central problem as described in Chapter 6, and find solutions as described in Chapter 7. We will now describe in more detail the steps in the process of helping a person to feel better.

THE HELPING PROCESS

Figure 5.1 describes diagrammatically the process that emerges when you use counselling skills in everyday conversations. The first part of the process has been described in previous chapters. If the troubled person accepts the initial and further invitations to talk, then the helper needs to actively listen while the person tells their story. During this active listening phase skills involving the use of short responses and reflection are invaluable. While actively listening, the helper needs to validate what the person is saying and to help them to recognise, own, and feel free to express their emotions.

In this chapter we will first discuss validation and then consider ways of helping a person to recognise, own and express emotions. Later, in Chapter 6, we will describe ways to help the person focus on the central problem and in Chapter 7 will explain how to help the person find solutions so that the process illustrated in Figure 5.1 is followed.

> Expressing emotions helps the person to change

Sometimes it is appropriate and satisfactory for a person who is being helped to finish the conversation after telling their story or after focusing on the central problem without continuing the rest of the process. We need to remember that everyday-life conversations need to finish when a comfortable point is reached. Sometimes it is sufficient for a person just to tell their story, as after this they may feel better. At other times they may be motivated to continue talking in order to find solutions.

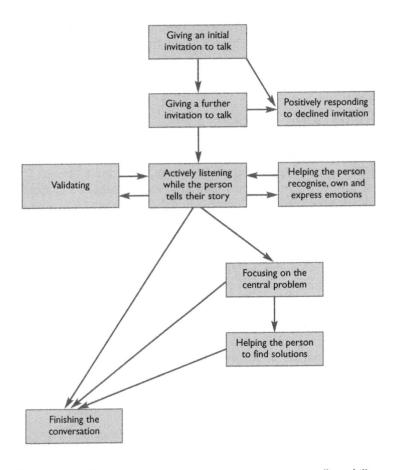

Figure 5.1 The process that emerges as you use counselling skills in everyday conversation

VALIDATION

Validation involves letting the person know that you have both heard and understood what they are telling you about themselves and their situation. When we validate we confirm that we are looking at the situation from the troubled person's perspective. We can do this in a number of ways.

First, we can use the skills we've discussed in the previous chapters. In particular the skills involved in actively listening give the person a message that we are listening and understand.

> Validation is like saying 'I can see what you are seeing'

As the person talks to us they effectively describe their situation as they see it. If we try to look through their eyes we will see the picture that they are painting of themselves and their situation. This picture may not be the same as our picture of them and their situation. We may have a different point of view. However, if we are to help them to feel better the first thing we need to do is to validate their picture so that they know that we understand their perspective fully. Trying to convince them that their picture is wrong will not be helpful; they need to be heard and understood. If you are to help them to feel better, you will need to convince them that you understand and respect their point of view. This is what we mean by validation.

You might validate a person's picture by saying something like:

I get the picture.

I understand what you are saying.

I can see what's happening for you.

I think I can understand how you might feel.

Note this last response wasn't, 'I know how you feel'. You cannot know how someone else feels; that's not possible. You are not that person, and if you say 'I know how you feel' then, to some extent, you invalidate the unique experience of that person.

Validation also involves letting the other person know that it is okay to feel the way they feel. We find that quite often a person will say, 'I shouldn't feel sad', or, 'I shouldn't feel angry', or, 'I shouldn't feel resentful'. The reality is that the person does feel that way and needs to be encouraged to accept the feeling as being legitimately theirs. In this situation a good response might be:

The reality is that you do feel resentful and, in my view, that's okay.

It seems to me that you do feel angry, and I think that in your situation I might feel the same.

You do feel sad and I can understand why.

By using these responses the person is encouraged to stay with their authentic emotional feelings instead of trying to disown them. This enables the person to deal with the feeling so that they can fully experience it. You may have noticed in yourself that when you fully experienced a feeling very often it will spontaneously diminish or change. If it doesn't, you then have the opportunity to do something to bring about some change in the feeling.

> When feelings are fully experienced they either diminish, or change into more comfortable feelings

As you will have recognised, validating is not about trying to change a person's picture which describes the way they see themselves and the world around them. It is about helping them to get fully in touch with and accept the picture that they have described. To some, this may seem to be a strange process to use when trying to help someone to feel better. They would prefer to try to help people to look on the bright side of life and see things from a more positive point of view. Although this is an admirable goal in the long term, the best way to achieve this is generally to stay with the person's current perspective so that they can deal with the associated emotions. Once they have done that they will be in a better position to move forward.

Some people may argue that this is not always the case because we know from common experience that some people who are troubled have a very distorted view of their situation. Therefore it might seem appropriate to challenge their distorted views. However, if we try to change a person's view by direct confrontation we are likely to alienate them and unfortunately, as a consequence, to reinforce their view. Paradoxically, if we are able to join with them, see their world from their point of view, and validate this, they are more likely to be able to shift in their perspective so that they feel better.

HELPING THE PERSON TO EXPRESS AND RELEASE EMOTIONS

Before discussing the expression and release of emotions it might be useful for us to tell you about Keith. Keith is a young man in his early 30s who is married with two children. He has recently discovered that his wife has an eye condition which will progressively become more serious. At present she has tunnel vision and in the future she is likely to lose her sight altogether. Not surprisingly, Keith is anxious and depressed. In the past he has been a very cheerful fellow who helped his colleagues in the office to feel good. For a week or two, his colleagues had noticed that he was saying very little and looking miserable. Eventually one of them, Madeleine, asked him what was troubling him, to which he replied, 'Nothing'. 'Cheer up then', said Madeleine. She was somewhat taken aback with what she thought was a very abrupt and rather disrespectful response.

With the best of intentions, Madeleine had failed to help her workmate. You might like to stop for a moment to think about what she might have done differently and jot down some notes here:

1. ....

2. ....

3. ....

Madeleine might have had more success if she had remembered that, as discussed in Chapter 3, we need to be very sensitive in inviting a person to talk. When someone is hurting they need to be approached carefully, because if they are not they are likely to withdraw into themselves and push other people away just as Keith did. It could also have been useful for Madeleine to have expressed her concern by letting Keith know that she had noticed how he had changed. She could have gently given him feedback as described in Chapter 3. Perhaps Madeleine's worst mistake was to tell Keith to cheer up. When someone is troubled it is extremely insensitive and counterproductive to suggest that they should somehow magically be able to put aside their negative feelings and feel better. Unfortunately it is common social practice in our society for us to use expressions like, 'Cheer up', 'Be positive', 'Things could be worse', and 'Don't worry, things will be okay'. Although such expressions often help the speaker to feel better, they are really of little use to the listener.

> 'Cheer up, be happy!' rarely works

What would have been more helpful for Keith would have been for Madeleine to have reflected back what she had noticed, to have expressed her concern and to have given an initial invitation for Keith to talk, as explained in Chapter 3. If Keith had responded positively she could have given a further invitation. She could have continued by using the skills described in Chapter 4 to give Keith an opportunity to tell her about his problem. In particular, she could have reflected back his emotional feelings. For example, she might have said:

You seem to be very sad as you talk about your wife losing her sight.

You're feeling very stressed by the situation.

You're worried about your wife.

You're angry because you think the doctors have failed her.

Depending on what Keith had said previously, any of these responses might have helped him to get in touch with his inner feelings. He might then have talked about how he felt more fully, or have openly expressed his feelings in some way. For example if Madeleine had noticed that he was sad and had reflected back that sadness, Keith might have started crying.

The tendency to avoid expression of emotional feelings

Commonly, in our social relationships with other people, human beings tend to avoid expression of emotional feelings. We often try to hide our own feelings, or in subtle ways invite other people to avoid expressing their feelings either by changing the subject or by giving them messages which suggest that they should feel better or think positively. Why do we do this? We probably do this because it is painful for us to get in touch with our own troubling emotions, and/or to listen to other people's troubling emotions. The problem is that if someone else tells you about their own sadness, disappointment, frustration or anger, you are likely to be brought in touch with similar emotions in yourself. This may be uncomfortable and/or painful for you. We need to remember though, that if we are to help people feel better we will need to give them an invitation and the opportunity to openly express troubling emotional feelings. As we have discussed, the best way to do this is to reflect back the feelings that we believe the person is experiencing.

> Openly expressing troubling emotional feelings provides relief and helps the person to feel better

Identifying and naming emotional feelings

As helpers, we need to recognise that many people have been brought up to deny what are generally described as negative feelings. These include sadness, frustration, anger and disappointment. How often have you heard a parent say to a child, 'Don't cry', or 'Don't be angry'?. As a consequence of messages such as these many people find it difficult in adult life to recognise, identify, own and name their emotional feelings, particularly when these are intense. When they start to recognise such feelings they try to push them away and if they can't do that, they try to hide them from other people. Consequently, when we are trying to help someone who has learnt to hide their feelings it is often useful for us to help them to identify and name their feelings.

A useful way to help other people to get in touch with their feelings is for the helper to share how they themselves might feel in the same situation. Consider the previous example concerning Keith and Madeleine. If Keith had told Madeleine about his wife's eye condition, he might just have shrugged his shoulders and said something like, 'That's life'. Madeleine might then have been able to help him get in touch with his sadness by saying, 'If I were in your situation I think that I would feel very sad'. There are a number of similar expressions which can be useful in helping a person to get in touch with and name emotional feelings. These include:

I guess I would feel ... (angry, frustrated, sad, disillusioned, and so on), if that had happened to me.

In the same situation I might feel ...

I think that a lot of people would feel ... if that had happened to them.

By making statements such as these the person concerned may be able to recognise their feelings and realise that these are legitimate. Consequently they may be able to fully own their feelings, and experience and express them, so that they feel better.

In helping other people to correctly identify their feelings it is useful to be familiar with the names of a wide range of different feelings. Additionally, it is an advantage if you are able to distinguish between different levels and types of emotional feeling.

Consider the following descriptions of emotional feelings:

wistful – disappointed – sad – distressed – distraught.

In some ways these fit along a continuum as they are similar but not quite the same. There are subtle differences in the qualities and intensity of the feelings described by these words. If we are to be good helpers we need to be familiar with a wide range of feeling words and their subtle differences so that we can accurately reflect feelings. If our attempts to name the other person's feelings are inaccurate, our reflection may still be useful, but clearly it will be most helpful if the words we use accurately identify the person's actual experience.

HELPING PEOPLE WHO ARE DISTRESSED AND CRYING

If somebody is distressed and crying then you need to decide whether to sit quietly and allow them to continue crying without interruption, or whether to interrupt their process. The question you need to ask yourself is, 'Can I cope with them crying?'. If you can, then it's good to allow them to cry so that they can fully express their sadness and start to feel better. The alternative is to recognise that the help you can give them is limited and to look after yourself.

If you want to be an effective helper then you will need to allow the other person to cry and may even encourage this by saying something like 'It doesn't trouble me when you cry', or, 'It's okay for me if you cry' (provided that this is true). By doing this you effectively give the person permission to cry.

Sitting without saying anything while a person cries quietly can be useful in helping them to feel better. To do this successfully you will need to remain grounded and calm so that the person concerned is aware of your empathic, supportive, but non-intrusive presence. Although sitting quietly in this way can be useful, sometimes it can be helpful if you ask the person concerned to describe in words the underlying reason for the tears. Often someone who starts to cry will be unable to say anything. However, after a while, you may be able to help them by asking about the reason for their tears. You might ask a question such as one of these:

Can you tell me what those tears are about?

Can you tell me what those tears are saying?

Can you put words to your tears?

By asking questions like these the person is invited to think about why they are crying. They may then be able to verbalise this so that they can deal with the relevant issues openly.

Should I comfort the person?

It is common for many people to believe that to help a person to feel better we should put our arms around them, pat them on the shoulder and tell them that everything will be alright. What do you think?

Clearly, there are differences of opinion about whether it is really helpful or not to comfort a distressed person by touching them or handing them tissues when they are crying.

In considering this question it is essential to respect personal, professional and ethical boundaries. People who are distressed are very vulnerable and some may be very needy because of their situation. It is highly unethical to take advantage of this vulnerability and neediness under the guise of comforting the person. Appropriate boundaries must be maintained. Compromising these will not help the person. It is likely to disempower them and may well be abusive so that in the future they will not seek or accept the help of others when they need it.

Generally, we believe that it is not helpful to comfort a distressed person except by being quietly present. Providing comfort by touching often intrudes on a person's ability to be able to continue talking and unloading what they need to express. Additionally, it may infringe the other person's boundaries. Obviously, exceptions to this rule apply to close relationships such as those which exist between partners and parents and their children.

> If you walk alongside a person you won't interrupt their journey

Trying to help a person to stop crying may give them a message that their story and distress is overwhelming you. If they get this message they are likely to stop talking about their problems in an attempt to look after your needs instead of theirs.

We believe it's important for the person being helped to retain confidence in their own sense of being in control of themselves. Even though they may at times lose this confidence, if they are allowed to cry it is likely that with time the crying will stop and they will realise that they do have control again. Where this doesn't happen, then help from a qualified and experienced counsellor or other professional is required.

PROTECTING YOURSELF FROM ABUSE

We all need to be very careful when helping people to get in touch with and express angry feelings. It is important to recognise that some people manage their anger inappropriately and can become violent. It is sensible to use your judgement in this regard. If you have any suspicion that the person you are trying to help may be unable to manage their anger appropriately, then it is not sensible to encourage them to express it. We suggest that you use extreme caution in this regard because strongly expressed anger can be very frightening, and people who do not know how to manage their anger appropriately can be dangerous. With such people it is obviously not sensible or helpful to encourage them to get in touch with and express their anger. Clearly, they need to learn ways to manage their anger appropriately, so you need to protect yourself and refer them to a counsellor or other professional who has the relevant training, experience and skills.

While recognising the need to protect ourselves from those who might become abusive towards us, we also need to recognise there are many people who do not engage in violent or other abusive behaviours. If you have confidence that the person you are helping can deal with their anger appropriately then it may be right for you to help them by reflecting their anger and allowing them to express it. As we have said, be cautious in this regard.

RECOGNISING YOUR OWN FEELINGS

Expression of strong emotion will inevitably have an impact on you if you try to be a helper for others. What will it be like for you? Consider what your initial reaction might be if your friend or colleague starts to cry while telling you something sad. You may feel like helping them to stop crying and take them away from their

97

distress. That's a perfectly natural response and reaction. It's exactly what everybody is taught to do from childhood. If someone is crying, comfort them. Tell them to stop crying, it's okay. Unfortunately, although that may help you feel better, it is not really helpful for them.

When we say to someone, 'Stop crying', what we do is comfort them and make them feel better in the short term, but we allow them to avoid facing the troubling issues which are causing their pain. By helping them to avoid those issues all we are doing is encouraging them to push the issues to one side and they are certain to bubble up again. Clearly, if you really want to help it is not useful to encourage people to bottle up emotions. Instead, we need to allow them to ventilate their feelings so that they can leave them behind and move forwards. This means that we are going to be confronted by people who cry, people who are despairing, people who are disillusioned, people who are angry and people with a range of other emotions. At times, it may be very difficult for us to cope with our own feelings when we are confronted by such situations.

One of the consequences of inviting a person to express their emotions is that they are likely to get more fully in touch with their feelings. When they do this those feelings may become more intense and they may express them in a very open way. For example if I had noticed that somebody, like Keith, was looking very sad and reflected back that sadness by saying, 'You look sad', the person might start to cry. If I say to somebody, 'You sound angry', I may be met by a very angry response. Funnily enough, quite often someone who is angry will respond by saying very angrily 'I'm not angry'. By doing this they may well feel better as a consequence of giving an angry response.

We know that if we are to help someone feel better we need to be able to give them an invitation and the opportunity to fully express their troubling feelings in a way that is okay for them. As helpers, our problem is that if we do this we may also experience strong and possibly painful emotions ourselves. This is why we talk about people 'unloading' their feelings. Metaphorically speaking what the person we are helping does is to unload their feelings from their own shoulders. Some of these will fall to the ground, but inevitably some of them may land on our shoulders and trigger off feelings of our own. Clearly, the process of unloading troubling feelings is a cathartic and healing process for the person being helped. However, even if the helper is very well grounded they will at times be affected emotionally by listening to other people's problems. We strongly suggest that you read Chapter 10 in this regard so that you can look after your own needs.

Dealing with your own feelings while helping the other person

If you have joined with the person you are helping, and are seeing their world from their perspective, you are vulnerable with regard to catching their emotions.

> Emotions are contagious!

This raises the question, if you are helping someone who is very sad and cries, are you going to burst into tears as well? How will you deal with your own emotions in a situation like this? One way is to let the person know that what they have said also makes you feel sad. However, unlike the person who is crying, you need, if possible, to be able to give a message that you are not over-whelmed by what they are telling you. Sometimes you may be so affected that you do shed some tears yourself; after all you are a caring, sensitive human being. However, it is best if you are able to give the impression that you can cope, and are not overly distressed by what you are hearing. The problem is that if you can't do this the person who is being helped might think, 'Oh dear, I'm really distressing this person by what I am saying. I don't think I'd better tell them the rest of my story because they might fall apart.' Instead of being able to focus on their own problem, they might feel guilty for upsetting you!

We do need to be real when we are helping others. So rather than suppress our own emotional feelings altogether, we might express them in a caring way by saying something like:

I'm really saddened by what you have told me

or

I feel quite touched by what you said.

However, it is important to give the impression that it's okay for you to listen to the other person's story, even if it is an emotionally charged story. After you have helped someone express strong emotions you will need to look after yourself as described in Chapter 10.

chapter summary

- To start a change process we need to:
  - Actively listen.
  - Validate.
  - Help the person recognise, own and express emotions.

- To continue the change process we need to help the person to:
  - Focus on the central problem.
  - Find solutions.

- Validation involves letting the person know that we have heard, understood and are looking at the situation from their perspective.

- Openly expressing emotions provides relief and helps the person to feel better.

- It can be useful to help the person identify and name their emotional feelings.

- Words used to describe emotional feelings have subtle differences in meaning and intensity.

- Generally, it is more helpful to allow a person to cry than to interrupt their crying by trying to comfort them.

- Be aware that some people do not manage their anger appropriately, so you need to protect yourself.

- You need to recognise and deal with your own feelings (also see Chapter 10).

ASSIGNMENT EXERCISES FOR COURSEWORK STUDENTS

1. The words 'uneasy' and 'furious', and 'concerned' and 'distraught' are at opposite ends of a continuum in terms of emotional quality and intensity. On the lines below fill in the blank spaces with words which fit between those given. Additionally, complete all of the blank spaces below with other 'feeling' word continuums of your own choice.

uneasy	_____	_____	_____	furious
concerned	_____	_____	_____	distraught
_____	_____	_____	_____	_____
_____	_____	_____	_____	_____
_____	_____	_____	_____	_____
_____	_____	_____	_____	_____
_____	_____	_____	_____	_____
_____	_____	_____	_____	_____

2. Describe three situations, either real or imagined, which could arise in your own life but are as described below, in which a person who is talking to you might start to cry:

   a. A situation where it is acceptable for the person to cry.

   b. A situation where the person begins to cry but you realise that it is uncomfortable for them in that environment.

   c. A situation where the person starts to cry but you feel uncomfortable because they are crying.

   In each case describe the environment or situation, your relationship with the person, what you would say to the person, how you would manage the situation, and how you think you would feel. Comment on why you think the way you chose to manage the situation would be helpful for the person. Also, describe how you would relate to the person the next time you met them.

6 Focusing on the central problem

You might like to stop for a moment to think about the skills that we have discussed so far. We've talked about ways in which we can join with a person by listening attentively. We've talked about the way in which we can use short responses, that is expressions like, 'Ah hum', 'Yes', and 'Ah ha', to let the person know that we are listening. We have discussed the way in which we can let the person know that we are listening and understanding by reflecting back in our own words the things that have been said. We have also discussed the way in which we can identify emotional feelings and reflect those back so that the person can get more fully in touch with their emotions and deal with them. All of the skills we have discussed so far enable us to join with the person and to encourage them to continue talking about their problems.

While you are helping someone by using the skills we've discussed, try to imagine that you are the other person, with their problems, in their situation, seeing the world through their eyes. If you do this, you will be able to experience something of what it feels like to be them.

As you listen to the person's story, you may find that they are unable to think clearly about their situation because they are confused by many different thoughts and feelings that are buzzing around in their head. This is commonly the case. Just listening to them will be useful, but if you are to be of further help you will need to use your skills in a way which will enable the person to sort through their confusing thoughts so that they can focus more clearly on the most important issue or issues which are troubling them.

Often, the most important problem that is troubling a person is not the most obvious problem that the person initially talks about, but one that may be hidden behind other issues. However, with skill, you will be able to help the person identify the most troubling issue or issues and to bring these into focus so that they can be addressed.

HELPING THE PERSON TO FOCUS ON THEIR CENTRAL PROBLEM

Figure 6.1 illustrates the way a helpful conversation evolves. In this figure you will notice that in the right hand column we have identified three different points suitable for finishing a helpful conversation and have labelled these points as A, B, and C. It is up to you as the helper to make sensible decisions about when to finish a conversation. Remember, however, that if you try to continue a conversation beyond a point that is comfortable for the other person you may be intrusive and damage the relationship.

If you use the Rogerian skills described in earlier chapters you will give the other person the opportunity to share their story and describe their problems. As a consequence, they are likely to feel understood and may well feel better. Thus, in many situations it is appropriate to finish a conversation at point A, particularly when the issues are fairly minor.

Sometimes it will be more appropriate to continue the conversation and it may be clear that the person you're trying to help would like to do that. In this case, by continuing to use the active listening skills described previously, you may be able to help the person to get in touch with, and release, strong emotions. Once again, you have reached a point in the conversation where it may be appropriate to finish (point B). After releasing emotions, the person is likely to feel relieved and more comfortable.

If we finish the conversation at a point which is satisfactory for the other person, then it is quite possible that if they wish to explore their issue further that they will return to talk with us at another time. Alternatively, having started to explore the issue with us, they may feel that it is more sensible for them to continue by talking with a qualified counsellor. We ourselves like to see each conversation as a step up a flight of stairs. If we are able to help the person move up one step, we have certainly helped them in a process which might continue so that they find ways of leading a more comfortable and satisfying life in the future.

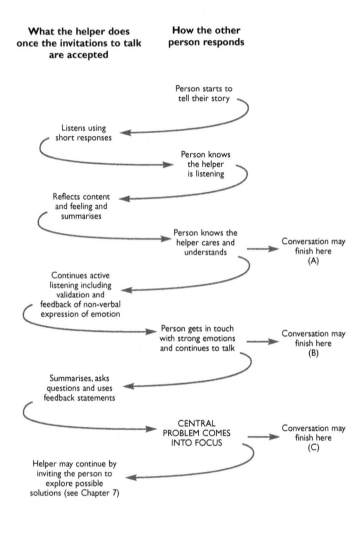

Figure 6.1 Helping the person to focus on the central problem

> One step today, another some time later

The skills that we have previously discussed may enable the person we are helping to spontaneously move to a point where the central problem which is troubling them comes into focus. However, for other people this may not be the case. They may find that although they feel better having talked about their problems and expressed emotions, they are still confused and unable to clearly identify their central problem. In this case it may be advantageous to use some additional skills to help them to focus on their central problem. However, we strongly suggest that you continue to rely heavily on the previously described skills, but supplement these with the following additional skills:

● Summarising
● Asking questions
● Use of feedback statements.

We will deal with each of the above in turn.

SUMMARISING

We will use an analogy to help us describe the counselling process. Imagine that the person who is talking to you, instead of talking, paints a picture of their problems for you on a blank canvas. Colours, shapes, lines and images start to appear on the canvas. As a few brush strokes are made you might just acknowledge that you have noticed these. Similarly, when counselling you might let the person who is being helped know that you're listening by using short responses, as discussed earlier.

As more brush strokes are made and shapes are created in the picture, you can let the artist know that you recognise what these shapes represent. Similarly, you can confirm that you understand what the person is telling you by using reflection of content. Also you can confirm that you understand how the person is feeling emotionally, by reflecting feelings.

As the picture continues to develop, several shapes might start to relate to each other, to overlap and interact with each other. When this happens, once again, you can let the person who is painting the picture know that you are recognising the picture and have some understanding of what it might be like to be in that picture. To do this you need to describe to the person what you see. Similarly, you can let the person know that you understand their situation by giving them a brief *summary* or description of a significant part of what they have told you.

A summary draws together the most important parts of what the person has told you and may also include mention of the person's feelings. Summaries can be made repeatedly during a conversation, at points where it would be useful to draw together ideas which have been expressed. By summarising, you present the person with a clearer picture by drawing out the most important facets of what they are saying so that they can focus more clearly.

> A summary helps the person to focus on what is important

It may be useful for you to use summarising several times in one conversation. Each time you summarise, the person being helped will be likely to see their overall picture more clearly and as a consequence will be likely to continue talking in a more focused way. At times, a summary will trigger off other feelings and thoughts, and the person may talk about these. However, finally you can summarise the overall picture after having previously summarised several of the smaller parts of the picture.

To make the process clearer, here are some examples of summaries. Notice that in each case the summary is used after several short responses or reflections have been used.

EXAMPLE I

This conversation took place in a tennis club after a game of tennis had finished:

Dennis: 'I'm really sorry Mary about the noise and trouble that John created while we were playing tennis. He's eight years old now and he should be able to behave a bit better than that. I'm really worried about him. He doesn't seem to be doing as he's told at all.'

Mary (the helper): 'You seem to be really worried about his behaviour.' (Reflection of feeling and content.)

Dennis: 'Yes, I am worried about his behaviour; I really don't know what to do about it. He's causing me a lot of problems and it's a worry. As you know I got married again last year and Jane, my new wife, finds it extremely difficult to cope with John's behaviour.'

Mary: 'Jane's having difficulty managing John.' (Reflection of content, which turned out to be inaccurate, but was still helpful in encouraging Dennis to continue talking.)

Dennis: 'Well, it's not so much that, it causes a few arguments between Jane and me. Jane thinks that I should be much firmer with John, and that I let him get away with things.'

Mary: 'Jane would like you to be a much firmer parent.' (Reflection of content.)

Dennis: 'Yes, Jane thinks I'm too soft. She is really getting quite angry with me because she blames me for John's behaviour at home and I just don't know what to do about it.'

Mary: 'It sounds to me as though you and Jane have different ideas about parenting John, and you're feeling worried about how the two of you are going to find a solution.' (*Summary.*)

Do you notice how the final summary focuses on the differences between the ways in which Dennis and Jane parent John? It doesn't focus on John's behaviour, instead it focuses on what is really troubling Dennis, and this concerns his relationship with Jane. What has happened is that Mary has succeeded, by using the active listening skills of reflection, in helping Dennis to identify the central problem which is troubling him instead of focusing on the presenting problem, which was John's behaviour.

EXAMPLE 2

Nancy and Margaret have the following conversation at their place of work:

Margaret: 'I'm sorry that I wasn't much help in that meeting Nancy. I've got a lot on my mind at the moment and I've got to come up with a decision fairly fast.'

Nancy (in a helping role): 'You're under a lot of pressure.' (Reflection of feeling – the feeling of being pressured.)

Margaret: 'Yes, I'm having trouble concentrating because I have to make a decision about what happens to my mother. She's quite elderly and lives alone quite a few miles from where I live.'

Nancy: 'Knowing that you have to make a decision seems to be worrying you.' (Reflection of content and feeling.)

Margaret: 'Yes, I suppose I have to make up my mind whether I invite her to come and live with us in our house, or whether I try and talk her into moving to a retirement village near where she lives now.'

Nancy: 'You've got a dilemma. You don't really know what to do. Whether to advise your mother to move in with you or to live somewhere else.' (*Summary.*)

EXAMPLE 3

This conversation takes place while Paul is visiting Marvin who is in hospital:

Marvin: 'I feel like discharging myself and getting out of this place right now.'

Paul (using helping responses): 'You're wanting to leave the hospital.' (Reflection of content.)

Marvin: 'Yes, I sure am, I think it's a bit risky in here. I'm scared stiff about what's going to happen.'

Paul: 'Uh-hm. (Short response.)

Marvin: 'I don't think I should have this operation at all. I think it's a big mistake.'

Paul: 'You're worried about this operation.' (Reflection of feelings and content.)

Marvin: 'Yes, I am. I think it might leave me disabled you know.'

Paul: 'Mm.' (Short response.)

Marvin: 'Maybe I'd be better off just staying with the problem rather than taking a big risk, like being disabled. This is just not good. I don't think I should have decided to come here in the first place.'

Paul: 'You're regretting having made the decision to come into the hospital for this operation.' (Reflection of feeling and content.)

Marvin: 'Yes, I am regretting making that decision.'

(Marvin pauses, and Paul remains silent because he can see that Marvin is thinking.)

Marvin: 'Although I'm not sure whether I am or not. I can't make my mind up. You see, it's really a bit complicated.'

Paul: 'Yes.' (Short response.)

Marvin: 'I think there is more to it than just having the operation.'

Paul: 'You sound confused about why you've come into hospital.' (Reflection of feeling and content.)

Marvin: 'Yes. I am confused, I don't think I thought through the issues properly, and there are lots of issues that I need to take into account. I haven't considered the implications of the operation properly.'

Paul: 'You didn't think things through fully before you made the decision to come into hospital.' (Reflection of content.)

Marvin: 'No, I didn't. I should have thought about the implications for the kids. You know if I come out of hospital and I'm paralysed, how am I going to look after them? I won't be able to.'

Paul: 'You've talked about your worry about having this operation and the implications for your children. It seems to me that you are still uncertain about the decision you've made.' (*Summary.*)

Notice how Paul continually used reflection to allow Marvin to change his focus onto what was most important for him. Marvin started to talk about his fear of the operation, but moved on to talking about his concerns with regard to his children. Paul could have blocked Marvin from exploring the fears relating to his children if he had focused on Marvin's fear of the operation. However, instead of doing this, Paul continued to use reflection which encouraged Marvin to keep talking and enabled Paul to follow where Marvin went, so that eventually the central issue emerged. This example demonstrates the need to leave it open for the person being helped to move wherever they want to go, instead of the helper trying to control the direction of the conversation. Otherwise, new and underlying issues will be missed and, most importantly, the central problem may never be identified and addressed.

EXAMPLE 4

Jim: 'I seem to spend a lot of time on my own lately since I separated from my girlfriend.'

Max (using helping responses): 'Ah ha.' (Short response.)

Jim: 'I go out by myself and I see other people walking around together or in groups.'

Max: 'You sounded sad when you said that.' (Reflection of feeling.)

Jim: 'Yeah, it does make me sad. Wish that I had somebody to be with.'

Max: 'You're very alone.' (Reflection of content.)

Jim: 'Yes, I do feel lonely, especially in the evenings. I just sit at home and watch television by myself. I don't even do anything. I haven't got an interest or a hobby. I don't know what's the matter with me.'

Max: 'You seem to be worried about yourself because you're not motivated.' (Reflection of feeling and content.)

Jim: 'Yes, I am. I don't have any energy. I'm not particularly interested in anything. I don't have any idea what I could do. I just feel like a big blob.'

Max: 'You feel bad about yourself and you're not doing anything.' (Reflection of feeling and content.)

Jim: 'Yeah, I'm just a nothing. Why would anybody want to be interested in me anyway? I don't do anything.'

Max: 'What you've told me is that you're feeling lonely, and you recognise that you don't do things or go out because you don't feel good about yourself.' (*Summary.*)

The summaries which we have given above are quite short because they summarise only a short part of a counselling conversation. However, after a lengthy conversation, a summary might be longer. What is important is that the summary should enable the person to understand and recognise their issues. Here is an example of a typical summary which might be given after a person has talked for a while:

> *You have talked about a number of issues relating to working here. I've noticed that several times you have gone back to talking about your relationship with Phillip, your boss. You seem to be ambivalent about whether that relationship should be strictly a work relationship where you attend purely to the tasks which are part of your job, or whether you should explore the possibility of the relationship developing into a friendship.*

Do you notice how this summary makes things clearer by drawing attention to a recurring issue thus enabling the person to recognise what may be the most important part of what they are saying?

Using the skills learnt so far

Can you see how we could conduct quite a long and helpful conversation just by using short responses, reflection and summarising? These were the main methods used by Carl Rogers who, as we explained previously, pioneered *person-centred counselling*.

ASKING QUESTIONS

Have you noticed that up to now we have not mentioned using questions? This is because generally is not necessary to use questions in order to enable someone to talk about their problems. In fact, using questions is often unhelpful as it interrupts the flow of the conversation. What is worse is that questions may deflect the person away from the most important issues which concern them, and instead focus on things of interest to the person who is trying to help. Having said this, we do need to recognise that the use of relevant questions when appropriate can be helpful in enabling a person to focus on their central problem. However, questions do need to be used sparingly and with care. If they are used too frequently we will encounter the problems described before; the conversation will not flow smoothly as the questions will interrupt the natural process instead of allowing the person being helped to choose the path they wish to follow.

As a person talks with you, you will develop a mental picture of them and their life situation. As this picture develops, you may recognise that it is incomplete as parts of the picture are missing. Some information which you would like to know in order to complete the picture may not have been shared with you. It may be that, although it would be interesting for you to have the information which is missing, this information is not essential and you can continue the conversation without having the missing details.

Asking for information unnecessarily

Having a desire to help other people does not give us justification for prying into their lives unnecessarily. If you ask for information merely in order to satisfy your own curiosity and a desire to get a complete picture, you will be putting your own needs ahead of those of the person you're trying to help. This will not help them in any way. It is respectful to avoid asking for information, unless that information is critical to your understanding of the other person's problem. Additionally, it is worth noting that you will intrude on the person's ability to tell their story in their own way and without interruption, if you ask unnecessary questions.

> Avoid the temptation to ask unnecessary questions

We must admit that it can be very tempting to ask questions unnecessarily, and to try to focus the conversation on things that are of particular interest to us. In our experience this is a mistake. Often the things that are of interest to us will not be the things that are really troubling the person we're trying to help. Also, if we encourage someone to stay with the problem with which they initially present, then we may miss a much more important problem which underlies the presenting problem. We therefore need to be able to allow the person to go wherever they wish in telling their story. If we do this, then underlying issues, problems and feelings are likely to emerge. If we remember to walk alongside the person wherever they may wish to walk we are more likely to help them than if we take them on the journey which is directed by us. Clearly, asking unnecessary questions interferes with a person's ability to walk freely in their own direction.

Another problem is that if you were to ask too many questions the conversation would turn out to be more like an interview or interrogation than a natural conversation. If you find yourself asking too many questions, then pull yourself up, ask yourself whether you really need to keep using questions, and if not, then return to using the more reflective techniques which we have described previously.

> Ask as few questions as possible but make the questions you do ask really useful

When are questions useful?

Questions are particularly useful for the following purposes:

1. To help the person focus on their central problem.
2. To help the person continue telling their story.
3. To help you gain a fuller understanding of a person's situation.

Use of questions to help a person focus on their central problem

Having strongly advised against an over-reliance on questions, we need to recognise that questions can be extremely useful in helping a person to focus on the most important issues that are troubling them. We will illustrate this by using some examples.

Laurie and the human resources manager

Laurie is in a middle-management position in a large international corporation. He is highly regarded as a capable manager who is good at motivating his staff. He made an appointment to see the senior human resources manager, Fiona. It was clear to Fiona from the outset of the interview that something was troubling Laurie. She listened to him, using the active listening skills described previously, and noticed that he seemed to be unable to focus on one issue. However, several times he referred in a disparaging way to his relationship with another manager at the same level as himself, called Charles. Each time that he mentioned his relationship with Charles he seemed to become more anxious, and then deflected away to talk about something else which seemed to trouble him less. Fiona suspected that Laurie's central problem related to his relationship with Charles so made a feedback statement followed by the following question:

I have noticed that several times you have mentioned your relationship with Charles. Would you like to tell me more about that relationship?

In response to this question, Laurie told Fiona that he found it difficult to talk about the relationship because although he was having difficulty with Charles he felt a sense of loyalty to him. Using active listening skills Fiona was able to help him deal with his emotional feelings which were preventing him from talking about his central problem which did relate to his relationship with Charles.

Can you see how Fiona was able to help Laurie focus on his central problem by giving him feedback, followed up by a question which invited him to talk about the problem which was troubling him most?

Andrea and Mrs Burstall

Andrea works as a community nurse and one of her patients, Mrs Burstall, is an elderly lady who is confined to bed as a result of a chronic medical condition. She has a number of dressings which currently need to be changed regularly, and it is Andrea's job to do this. While attending to the medical needs this week, Andrea found that the patient, who is normally fairly comfortable emotionally, seemed to be troubled. Andrea gave her an invitation to talk, as explained previously, and Mrs Burstall began to talk about a number of issues that were worrying her. During the conversation Andrea used active listening skills, including short responses and reflection. Additionally, Andrea summarised what she had been told as follows:

You have talked to me about your son being unemployed, your daughter having difficulty looking after the children, your brother's alcohol problem, and the way your husband has problems repairing the house.

In response to this summary, Mrs Burstall agreed that there were a number of things worrying her. Andrea could have left the conversation there. However, she sensed that Mrs Burstall had avoided talking about her central issue. What she had done was to talk about other people's problems, and not her own response to these. Andrea therefore continued by asking the following question:

How do you feel emotionally when you talk about these problems?

By asking a direct question about Mrs Burstall's own feelings, Andrea was able to help her patient get in touch with her feelings of helplessness, and her sadness with regard to her inability to help the people she loved. Thus, she was enabled to focus on her central problem. Notice what Andrea didn't do, and what she did do. Andrea didn't invite Mrs Burstall to continue talking about other people's problems, because to do so would have deflected her away from her own issues. What she did do was to use a question to invite Mrs Burstall to talk about her own feelings when she talked about her relatives' problems. By doing this Mrs Burstall was enabled to explore her own issues rather than talk about other people's issues.

Use of questions to help a person continue telling their story

Questions can be used to help a person to continue talking, particularly when they appear to have difficulty in doing this. For example, a good way to encourage a person to continue exploring an important and troubling issue is to ask a question such as:

> *Would you like to tell me more ... (about your family or whatever)?*

Often questions such as the following will be sufficient to help the person to continue:

> *Is there anything else you would like to tell me?*

> *Would you like to expand on what you have said?*

Naturally, before asking questions like these we need to be sensitive to the needs of the other person. If we have joined with them effectively we will know whether or not it is appropriate for us to invite them to continue talking. If it isn't, we might use reflection to say something like:

> *It seems to be too hard for you to talk at the present time.*

Use of questions to gain a fuller understanding of a person's situation

Sometimes you won't be able to understand or make sense of a person's situation without having further information. In this case, it is sensible to ask a question, because by fully understanding how they picture their situation you will be in a better position to help them to sort out their problems.

At other times, you may find that you are becoming confused by a person's story. There may be things which just do not make sense to you. When this happens, you will need to ask a question so that you can understand the person's story and will be able to help them to focus on their most important issues. For example, a young woman may have given you the impression that her partner is the father of her child, but may then add details which suggest that her partner is not the father of her child. This may make it impossible for you to make sense of her story. Clearly, in this case it might be appropriate to ask a question such as:

I'm confused, is the father of your child a different person from your partner?

Notice that this question starts with a statement of your own confusion. Thus, the person concerned is told that you are seeking the information so that you can understand her story, and not just to satisfy your own curiosity.

Types of question

In order to use questions effectively we need to understand the difference between open and closed questions. Both types of question are useful but for different purposes.

Open and closed questions

Closed questions are those questions which lead to a specific answer such as 'Yes', 'No', or where the response is specific. Here are some examples of closed questions:

1. Do you have any children?
2. Is your job satisfying?
3. Do you love your wife?
4. How old are you?

If you think about the answers which you might get to any of the above questions, you will realise that these questions are likely to elicit a short, specific answer. For example the answers to these questions could be:

- No
- Yes
- Yes
- 35.

Unfortunately closed questions like these invite a short answer and don't encourage the person to talk freely. However, we could ask for the same information in a different way, by using open questions such as these:

1. Would you like to tell me about your family?
2. Can you tell me about your job?
3. What sort of relationship do you have with your wife?
4. What can you tell me about your age?

What do you think the answers might be to the open questions listed above? Would they be the same or different from the answers to the closed questions?

> Open questions invite the person to talk more freely

You may have noticed that in answering the open questions the person would be likely to talk more freely and to give more expansive answers. Additionally, some unexpected information might arise in response to the open questions. Closed questions invite a specific short answer, whereas open questions invite the person to expand on their answer and to continue talking.

Consider the closed question, 'Do you like your job'. That question could well have resulted in the reply, 'No', and that might have been the complete reply. However, by asking the open question, 'What can you tell me about your job?', you might get a much richer response, including information about where the person works, what environment they work in, what type of work they do, how they feel about that work and information about the people at the work place and relationships with them. Consequently the open question not only allows the person to continue talking but also allows them to go in whatever direction is most important for them.

The problem with closed questions is that generally they close the person's options and discourage them from expanding on their answer and talking further. Clearly, if we want to help a person we need to use skills which encourage them to talk and expand on what they are saying so that we have a full description of their problems and issues. This means that, generally, open questions are more useful than closed questions. However, there are instances where closed questions are appropriate because we require a specific answer.

Because open questions are generally more useful, you may want to try to convert the list of closed questions below to open questions. A suggested list of suitable open questions is given at the end of the chapter. You might like to compare your own suggestions to these.

Practice examples (convert closed questions to open questions)

1. Do you have any children?
2. Do you and your partner argue frequently?
3. Is your elderly mother independent?
4. Do you like looking after your father?
5. Have you enjoyed being at work this week?
6. Is your son disobedient all the time?
7. Do you feel sad when you think about your aunt?

'Why', 'what' and 'how' questions

Perhaps the most common types of question used in everyday life start with 'why', 'what', and 'how', so let's think about these types of question.

Generally, 'why' questions are not terribly helpful or useful. A person who has been asked a question beginning with 'why' will tend to respond with explanations instead of staying with their emotional feelings and thoughts. For example, imagine that we asked somebody, 'Why did you leave your husband?'. The person is likely to respond by telling us several reasons why they left. However, that has little relevance to the issues which might be troubling them now as a consequence of leaving. By asking the 'why' question, what we would have done would have been to divert them into talking about past history rather than into talking about how the issues affect them personally now.

Rather than starting questions with 'why', it is usually better to start them with words such as 'what' and 'how'. If you think back to the previous example, instead of asking a 'why' question, we might have asked the question:

How do you feel now that you have left your husband?

or

What is it like for you now that you have left your husband?

Notice that the second question includes the words 'for you', because it is important for the person to focus on their own feelings rather than just talk about things generally. Also notice that both questions relate to the person's feelings *in the present* rather than in the past. To be helpful, it is important for us to encourage people to talk about their current experiences, because it is in the present that they experience their pain.

Here are some examples of 'what' and 'how' questions which we might use:

What do you experience emotionally when you talk about this?

What might happen if you did that?

What options do you think you have? (see Chapter 7 regarding helping the person to find answers to problems)

How do you feel emotionally when you tell me ... ?

How does that affect you?

How are you feeling right now?

How would you know if ... (your mother was worried)?

How do you think you could change this situation?

THE USE OF FEEDBACK STATEMENTS

Statements can be very useful in giving feedback to a person and can help them to focus more clearly on what is important. Here are examples of useful feedback statements:

You seem to be having difficulty in describing this.

You seem to be stuck.

It's too difficult for you to make a decision.

Can you see what these feedback statements do? They feed back to the person something which you have noticed is happening as the person talks. This is useful, because it enables the person to stop, think and focus more intently on what is happening to them as they talk.

For example a person might continually refer to an incident regarding sexual harassment at work, move away from talking about it, then return to it, only to move away again. In this case we might use a feedback statement to say:

I notice that you have several times referred to an incident of sexual harassment, but each time have moved away from talking about it.

This feedback statement accurately describes what has occurred without interpretation. It helps the person to recognise what they are doing and enables them to make a decision about whether to talk about that sexual harassment more fully or whether to say, 'I don't want to talk about it'.

MAKING USE OF VARIOUS SKILLS

Let us look at an example of part of a counselling conversation where the skills of using short responses, reflecting, summarising, questioning, and giving feedback statements, are all included.

Mike (who makes use of counselling skills): 'How are you today?'

Bob: 'Not so good Mike.'

Mike: 'I'm sorry to hear that. Would you like to tell me what's troubling you, or would you prefer not to talk about things?' (Question.)

Bob: 'Yeah, I'm a little bit worried about how things are going.'

Mike: 'Uh ha.' (Short response.)

Bob: 'You know that we've just moved into a new house down on the south side of the city.'

Mike: 'Yes.' (Short response.)

Bob: 'Well I'm not finding it very easy to make friends with any of the people down there.'

Mike: 'You seem to be worried about that.' (Reflection of feeling.)

Bob: 'Yeah, well I am. Mary, as you know, was reluctant to move house in the first place and go down that way, and I suppose with me not being able to get on with the neighbours and people in our street, things are a bit difficult.'

Mike: 'It's hard for you.' (Reflection.)

Bob: 'Yeah, it is hard. I don't know what's wrong with me. We were able to move down there because, you know, they paid me out at work, so I had a fair wad of money to buy the new house with. But, even though we've got a really good house, I just don't get any satisfaction out of being there.'

Mike: 'You made a big decision and you're not feeling very positive about the outcome.' (Reflection of content and feeling.)

Bob: 'No I'm not and it's not getting any better. Like I've tried to invite people over and have a chat with the guy next door, but they're not the kind of people that I'm used to.'

Mike: 'You don't like them very much.' (Reflection of content.)

Bob: 'Well, I just don't seem to be able to get on with them. I find myself not having anything to say to them; we don't have anything in common and that doesn't make me feel good because I'm a person who gets along with everybody usually.'

Mike: 'However, right now you're having trouble getting along with these new neighbours.' (Reflection of content.)

Bob: 'Yeah, I am. I know that when I was at work, you know before I was retrenched, I used to get on with my boss, I used to get on with my workmates, I used to get on with the secretary. I didn't have trouble with any of those people. Gee, my boss was one of the best guys I ever knew and I didn't have any trouble talking to him.'

Mike: 'I get the impression that you're missing the people back at work.' (Reflection of content and feeling.)

Bob: 'Yeah, I am missing the people at work. I wish I was back there.'

Mike: 'There is a big loss for you.' (Reflection of content.)

Bob: 'Yeah, but I can't do anything about it now and I don't want to replace the people that I worked with, with these people here. They're not even like me.'

Mike: 'As I listen to you it seems to me that you are missing the people back at work and comparing them with the people here. I wonder what the difference is?' (Summary followed by a question.)

Bob: 'Well the difference is that I never really had to try too hard with the people at work. Conversations seemed to happen easily and there was a lot of joking. The people at work knew me, we used to have social get-togethers at work. I didn't have to explain very much about myself.'

Mike: 'It was all very natural and easy at work and now that's gone, and it's not the same where you are now.' (Short summary.)

Bob: 'Yeah, I feel a bit embarrassed because I wonder what the people around my neighbourhood might think of me.'

Mike: 'You sound unsure of yourself as a person and unsure about how other people see you.' (Feedback statement.)

Bob: 'Yeah, well, I'm not the same as I was, am I? I don't work any more. I haven't got a job. I'm in a new neighbourhood, so I don't have any friends.

Mike: 'You sound miserable when you say that.' (Feedback statement.)

Bob: 'I feel miserable. I just don't know who I am, what I can do any more, or what I'm good at.'

Mike: 'It's like you've lost your whole sense of identity.' (Feedback statement which moves Bob into a position where he can focus on his central problem.)

Bob: 'Yes I have, and I don't know what to do about it.'

We'll finish looking at this segment at this point, because the conversation is about to move into a new stage which is concerned with helping the person to find solutions to problems. This will be discussed in Chapter 7.

IN CONCLUSION

In this chapter we have discussed ideas, which you can use to help a person sort out their confusion and to focus more clearly on their most important issues or central problem. These ideas include the use of previously learnt skills, together with the use of summarising, asking questions and giving feedback statements.

Suggested open questions for practice examples (conversion of closed questions to open questions)

1. Can you tell me about your family?
2. What is your relationship like with your partner?
3. Can you tell me about your mother's ability to be independent?
4. What's it like, caring for your father?
5. What has it been like for you at work this week?
6. Can you tell me about your son's behaviour?
7. How do you feel when you think about your aunt?

chapter summary

■ The best way to help a person to tell their story is by actively listening, using reflection and summarising.

▓ To enable a person to focus on their central problem we may use the additional skills of asking questions and making feedback statements to supplement the basic reflective listening skills.

▓ A summary draws together the most important parts of what a person has said in a brief or a lengthy part of a counselling conversation.

▓ Questions should be used sparingly.

▓ Generally open questions are preferable because they invite the person to continue talking and exploring issues.

▓ 'What' and 'how' questions are more useful than 'why' questions.

▓ Feedback statements are helpful in raising a person's awareness of what is happening within themselves.

ASSIGNMENT EXERCISES FOR COURSEWORK STUDENTS

1. Imagine that you are having a conversation with a friend of yours called Howard who you would like to help. Howard has told you the following:

   He is 42 years old and for the past 20 years has worked as an engineer. He hates engineering and is studying anthropology on a part-time basis at the university. As a consequence of this he has financial difficulties, and his relationship with his wife has deteriorated. She's angry because he isn't continuing to work full-time in engineering. In his university course there are a number of single women who are relating in a very positive way to him. He is tempted to have an affair. He feels guilty about this, and is also guilty because his university commitments are preventing him from spending as much time with his children as he would like.

   How would you summarise this information for Howard? Explain how you believe that your summary would be useful to Howard.

2. Refer to the scenario described in Exercise 1, and imagine that you have summarised what Howard has told you. After hearing your summary, Howard continues to talk about the various issues that are troubling him. As he talks, you notice that he frequently mentions his wife's attitude, but that each time he does he quickly changes the subject to talk about something else.

   Explain three different ways in which you might help Howard to become more focused in his thinking. Give examples of the things you might say in each case.

7 Exploring possible solutions

Would you like to go back to the previous chapter and have another look at Figure 6.1? If you do, you will notice that in that figure we identified three positions A, B, and C, where it can be appropriate to finish a conversation without proceeding any further. We think that it is far more important to finish a conversation at a point which is comfortable for the other person rather than to continue with the aim of finding a solution. For example a person will often feel valued and helped if a conversation ends at point A, because at this stage they will have had an opportunity to tell their story and will feel understood. That may be all they need at that point in time. Similarly, if a conversation finishes at point B, the person is likely to feel better as they will have had a chance to get in touch with, and possibly release, emotions. Sometimes it is clear that a person would like to continue beyond that point, in which case it is useful to help them to identify their central problem more clearly as described in Chapter 6. Once again, it may be appropriate to finish the conversation at that point. Many people feel relieved when they clearly understand what is troubling them. Once they have done this, they may be satisfied for the time being, so it is not necessary to continue the conversation unless they wish to do that. Even so, there are other times when a person will be searching for a solution to their problem. In this case it is appropriate to continue the conversation so that they have the opportunity to explore possible solutions and decide what action to take.

> Be person focused so that the person can find their own solution

In writing this chapter, we remember that in Chapter 2 we suggested that the relationship is more important than the problem, and the person is more important than the solution. In our view, the most important part of a helping conversation is the first part which occurs as illustrated in Figure 6.1 up to point A. It is in this part of the conversation that the person is able to tell their story, and to feel valued and respected as you listen. A relationship of trust develops, and often it is not necessary to continue talking beyond point A. Certainly, we believe that it is usually unhelpful to try to focus on the central problem and help a person explore solutions early in a conversation. It is much more useful to give the person time to tell their story and get in touch with their emotional feelings before considering the possibility of moving on towards finding solutions.

THE SOLUTION MUST SUIT THE PERSON

Having cautioned against being solution focused rather than person focused, you may be interested to know that there is a modern approach to counselling called *solution-focused counselling*. While we believe that this is a valid approach, we do not think that it is generally of use in everyday conversations. However, it must be obvious that there are many situations where a person will gain considerable satisfaction if they are able to find solutions which fit for them. Consequently, it is useful for us, as people who wish to help other people in our daily lives, to learn skills which will enable us to help them find solutions to their problems. Notice that we have said, 'to help people find solutions to their problems'. We have not said that it would be useful for us to discover solutions to other people's problems, or to tell them what we believe would be the best solutions. We need to respect other people's abilities to find their own solutions, and we also need to recognise that the solutions that we ourselves would choose may not fit for the other person.

> Respect the person's right to make their own choices

Sometimes a person may choose a solution which we believe is inappropriate or undesirable. However, we need to respect their right to make their own choices. If we don't do this, we will disempower them so that they start to believe that they do not have the capacity to find their own solutions. Having said this, if a person decides on a solution which will quite clearly have detrimental effects on themselves or someone else, then we do have an ethical responsibility to draw their attention to the likely consequences. Initially we can do this by asking, 'What do you think the likely outcome might be?' and then if they are not able to recognise the problems inherent in their 'solution', we have an obligation to let them know what we think. In particular if the person's own safety, or someone else's safety, is likely to be compromised, or property is likely to be damaged, we have a moral obligation to take action to prevent this from happening.

How are we to set about the process of helping someone to explore possible solutions to their problem? Well, there are a number of useful ways of doing this. These include:

1. Giving the person time to find a solution.
2. Simply relying on the active listening and reflective skills previously described.
3. Inviting the person to think about alternatives and to think about what it would be like to use particular solutions.
4. Using a range of questions which are specifically intended to help people find solutions.

ENCOURAGING A PERSON TO TAKE TIME TO FIND A SOLUTION

You may be surprised to discover that our first suggestion in helping a person to find a solution to their problem is to invite them to take time to find their solution. We believe that this is probably the most important way in which you can help a person when they are struggling to solve a problem. Have you ever noticed what it is like for you yourself when you feel pressured to find the solution to a problem which is troubling you? In our experience the more pressured we feel, the less likely we are to find a solution which fits and works. Having said this, we do need to recognise that there are life-threatening crisis situations where an immediate decision is required. These cases are usually exceptional and if we have expertise relevant to a particular crisis situation, we may need to use it. For example, if you work as a paramedic and someone phones you to say that their relative is in a life-threatening situation, you have an obligation to give direct advice immediately so that the person concerned takes the most sensible and appropriate action. However, in everyday life, for most people, life-threatening situations are not regular occurrences, so generally the best rule is to give the person time to carefully consider their options.

When you are helping someone, stay in touch with your own emotional feelings. If you start to recognise that you are picking up the other person's feelings of panic and urgent need to find a solution, then pull yourself up. Slow down, and change the messages that you're giving yourself.

> Stay in touch with your own feelings

Instead of saying to yourself, 'I must help this person find a solution now', change the message into something like, 'It is not my job to find a solution to someone else's problem, and I need to remember that they may not be able to find their own solution right now'. In this regard, at times you may need to say to the person you are helping, 'You seem to be stuck and unable to find a solution right now. Maybe you will need more time to think things over.' By saying this you are reflecting back the reality. They can then recognise that they are stuck and may stop pressuring themselves to find an immediate solution. Most importantly, you will not make the mistake of trying to hurry them into solving their problem.

USING ACTIVE LISTENING SKILLS TO EXPLORE POSSIBLE SOLUTIONS

The skills described earlier in this book, which heavily emphasise reflection, are often sufficient in enabling a person to find a solution. We have found that if we reflect back what a person is telling us, and summarise from time to time, the person will often come to a point where they will find their own solution. Consider the following conversation between Kevin and Maria:

Kevin and Maria

Kevin told Maria that he was very troubled by a problem that had arisen at work. He is an accountant and in the course of his duties he has come across some anomalies in the company's accounting processes. He suspects that an accounting fraud is being perpetrated. This has put him in a dilemma. As he told his story, Maria continued reflecting back the content of what he was saying and his emotional feelings. After a while she summarised as follows:

Maria: 'Kevin, you've told me that you suspect that someone is involved in a fraudulent process and that the person concerned may be either one of your colleagues or your immediate line manager, or possibly his line manager. You're uncertain about whether to keep quiet for a while until you have more information, or whether to tell either your boss, his boss, or the chief executive officer of the company. Also, I notice that you seem to be very worried by the situation.'

Kevin: 'Yes, I do feel worried because if I wait before reporting what I suspect, I may be implicated myself. On the other hand, if I report the situation, I may be tipping off whoever it is who is perpetrating the fraud.'
(*Notice that Kevin is already starting to explore some options and the possible consequences of these.*)

Maria: 'You're worried that if you wait you may be implicated yourself.'

Kevin: 'Yes I am, and I can't afford to let that happen, because if it did my career would be ruined.'

Maria: 'You seem to be very clear in saying that you can't afford to wait.'
(*Here, Maria uses reflection to confirm a decision that Kevin has made.*)

Kevin: 'Yes I am, but I don't know who to talk to about my suspicions.'

Maria: 'You said that the possibilities were to talk to your boss, his boss, or the chief executive officer.'

Kevin: 'Yes I did, and now that you have pointed that out, I realise that there is another option. Because of the seriousness of the situation I could put my concerns in writing to my immediate supervisor with copies going to his manager and the chief executive officer. The only problem would be that I might be unpopular if I did, because I will have exposed the scam very publicly.'

Maria: 'You have discovered a possible solution, but it might be a costly one for you.'

Kevin: 'Yes it might, but I don't have an option, if I don't do that I won't sleep well at night. I know what I have to do, and I will do it.'

Even though Kevin knew that the solution might have negative consequences for him, he was relieved because he knew what he wanted to do. He had found his own solution. Notice that the only skills that Maria used were those of reflection and summarising. Frequently, these are the only skills that are needed. Using these skills alone has the advantage that the person being helped is certain to make a decision which fits for them.

You probably recognise that using this method of helping a person find a solution involves patience, as the helper needs to continue to reflect what the person is saying so that they can see their own situation more clearly and discover for themselves what they need to do. It does need to be recognised that some people may have difficulty in finding solutions when they are helped in this way because they are unable to think clearly about their options.

EXPLORING ALTERNATIVES

If you find that the person you're trying to help is keen to find a solution but is unable to do so in response to active listening, it may be appropriate for you to be more direct in helping them to explore alternatives. However, we recommend that you should be tentative in this process and remember that generally it is okay for someone to be stuck for a while before discovering solutions for themselves. You may need to tell them this by saying something such as, 'I know that you want to find a solution, but you seem to be stuck and unable to find one at the moment. Sometimes it is okay to wait for a while until you discover a solution, although I recognise that this may be hard for you to do.' Notice that this statement reflects back to the other person what you have observed, and also lets them know that sometimes it is okay to wait for a while until a solution emerges.

If the person concerned is still keen to look for possible solutions, then you may decide to help them to look at their options. Consider the case of Bob and Erica.

Bob and Erica

Erica has for some years been heavily involved in leadership activities in a Christian church. Bob is a close friend who doesn't share Erica's beliefs, as he is more inclined to live his life according to a Buddhist philosophy. Over the past few weeks Erica has talked with Bob about ongoing disagreements which she has been having with the pastor at the church and with other leaders in the church. With time, she has become progressively more distressed emotionally as a consequence of her experiences at her church. Erica has told Bob about her very strong religious beliefs and disagreement with some of the teachings and practices which are being promoted and used by the pastor and other leaders in the church. She explained that she has tried to put her point of view forward at a number of church meetings and has felt unsupported and sometimes attacked. She feels frustrated and angry because her views are not being respected. One day recently she talked with Bob about her problems. During this conversation Bob actively listened, reflecting content and feelings, and summarised. The conversation then continued as follows:

Erica: 'Yes Bob, the situation has been driving me crazy. I feel a lot calmer now that I have told you about my angry feelings, but I don't know what to do now. What do you think I should do?'

Bob: 'I don't know what you should do Erica, because I'm not you, but I'm wondering whether you think it would be helpful if we were to look at some options together?' (Gives an invitation to explore options together.)

Erica: 'I don't know what I could do, because my religious beliefs are important to me and I don't intend to let go of them.'

Bob: 'You seem to have made an important decision, not to let go of your beliefs.' (Reflection.)

Erica: 'Yes I have, but the tension at the church is starting to wear me down, I'm not sure what to do about that.'

Bob: 'What sort of things would need to happen so that you could feel better?' (Question to invite Erica to think of options.)

Erica: 'Well, I would feel better if they would accept my point of view.'

Bob: 'Okay, one option would be to try to convince them to change their beliefs.' (Reflection.)

Erica: 'They are never going to do that!'

Bob: 'So, if they're not going to change their point of view, what other options do you have?' (Invitation to look for other options.)

Erica: 'I could leave the church altogether.'

Bob: 'Are there any other things you could do?' (Invitation to look for other options.)

Erica: 'I don't know ... I suppose I could go and talk to the pastor about the way I feel.'

Bob: 'Have you any other ideas?' (Invitation to look for other options.)

Erica: (after thinking for a moment) 'I could write a letter and try to get it published in the church newsletter.'

Bob: 'Okay, you've suggested three options: leave the church, talk to the pastor, and write a letter to the church newsletter. Let's think about those. Can you imagine for a moment that

you've left the church? What would that be like for you?'
(Summary of options followed by exploration of one option.)

Erica: 'It would be terrible, I would lose too much. I belong
there, most of my friends are there, it's my spiritual base.'

Bob: 'Right now you don't seem ready to leave.' (Reflection.)

Erica: 'Well I've been thinking about leaving but I don't want to.'

Bob: 'So that leaves the other options, you could talk with the
pastor or write to the newsletter. What would it be like to talk
to the pastor?' (Exploration of one option.)

Erica: 'I'm a bit worried about talking to him. He's a nice fellow
but he does have very strong views.'

Bob: 'I get the impression that you feel intimidated by him.'
(Reflection.)

Erica: 'I'm not going to let that stop me! I'll go and talk to him.'

As you read through the above did you notice what Bob did? He
continued to listen and reflect while inviting Erica to look for
options. He was careful to try to avoid influencing Erica by putting
forward his own views or suggestions. Did you notice that he said,
'I don't know what you should do', early in the conversation?

> The person with the problem is the expert and is capable
> of finding their own solution

There are a number of different statements you can use to convey
the message that you are not the expert on what a solution should
be, but that the other person is. For example you might say:

I'm not sure what to suggest, what ideas do you have?

*I think it's important that whatever you decide fits for you.
What options do you see?*

*I am not comfortable telling you what to do, because you are
you, and I am me, and we are different, but I would be happy
to help you sort through some ideas.*

I can't advise you what to do, but I wonder whether you'd find it useful for us to talk together about some possible options?

There will be times when it is sensible to put forward an obvious suggestion which has been missed, but this needs to be done tentatively so that it doesn't seem like advice. For example, if Erica had been unable to think of any options, Bob might have said, 'It might not suit you, but I'm wondering whether you've considered talking to the pastor about your feelings?'. Notice the beginning of this suggestion, 'It might not suit you'. By saying this, the suggestion is made tentatively rather than as a recommended suggestion.

USEFUL QUESTIONS TO HELP IDENTIFY POSSIBLE SOLUTIONS

We need to caution against the premature use and/or overuse of questions. If they are used too early in a conversation the relationship is likely to be compromised, the person will not have an opportunity to fully explore their situation and tell their story, they may not feel valued, and may prematurely find a solution which, on reflection, they may realise is unsatisfactory for them. However, after using active listening skills with an emphasis on reflection and summarising, it may be helpful to use one or two questions in order to help them discover a solution to their problem. As we have explained in an earlier chapter, we need to be careful not to overuse questions because, if we do, the helping conversation will become more like an interrogation than a conversation and that will be uncomfortable for the person we're trying to help.

Questions which help to identify options

You may have noticed that in the conversation detailed earlier between Bob and Erica, Bob asked Erica a number of questions and these were useful in helping her move towards finding a solution. Useful questions include:

What sort of things would need to happen so that you could feel better?

What other options do you have?

COUNSELLING SKILLS IN EVERYDAY LIFE

Are there any other things you could do?

Have you any other ideas?

Are there any other ways for you to respond to that?

If the same situation arises in the next few days what do you think you will do? (Will you do this, or will you do that?)

What alternatives do you have?

EXPLORING THE CONSEQUENCES OF CHOOSING A PARTICULAR OPTION

As you will realise, the process of finding a solution usually involves the person concerned thinking about a number of options which are available to them. Once they have identified their options it can be useful to invite them to think about the consequences which might result from the choice of each option. In doing this, it is often best if the options are considered one at a time. A good way to do this is to invite the person to imagine that they have chosen a particular option, and to ask them how they would feel, and what the consequences might be. For example, you might ask:

Can you imagine that you have chosen to ... (reconcile with your wife)?

After asking this question, you can then use a follow-up question to explore what it would be like to have selected that option. For example you might ask:

What would that be like for you?

How would it feel if you chose to do that?

What would be the advantages and disadvantages of doing that?

What would be gained by doing that?

What would you lose by doing that?

Reluctance to accept loss

The last question in the above list is particularly relevant, because one of the things that frequently stops people from making choices is a reluctance to accept loss. Interestingly, when we make a choice there is almost always a loss involved. Even in the most practical day-to-day decisions, we are confronted by issues involving loss. For example, consider making a decision about whether to buy a new car or whether to stay with your existing vehicle. If you buy a new car, you will lose a sum of money which you might have spent on something pleasurable such as a holiday, whereas if you keep the old car you will lose the benefits of having a new car. Can you see how it is that when we make choices we usually have to except that we will lose something. As the old saying goes, 'You can't have your cake and eat it'.

CONSIDER THE LEAST DESIRABLE OPTION FIRST

When helping a person to sort through their options it is often useful to encourage them to deal with the least desirable option first. Naturally, this does require personal judgement. What you believe to be the least desirable option may not be what the other person thinks is the least desirable option. However, if you are able to help them eliminate those options which are least appealing, the decision-making process is made easier for them. Interestingly though, we have sometimes noticed to our surprise that a person will return to an option which they initially considered to be undesirable. They may end up choosing this as their preferred solution, so be careful to retain an open mind and encourage the person you're helping to feel free to return to options which they have previously discarded.

DEALING WITH YOUR OWN FEELINGS

Often you will be successful in enabling a person to find a solution which suits them. When this happens you are likely to feel satisfied at the end of the conversation. At other times, the outcome will be different. Although the person you are trying to help may wish to find a solution, they may be unable to do so. In this case it is important for you to help them to feel okay about being stuck, and to remind them that, if that is the case, they may not need to rush into making the decision. However, we know from our own experience that sometimes this can be uncomfortable for a helper, particularly when it seems to the helper that there is an obvious and sensible solution.

It is always important for a helper to stay in touch with their own feelings, and this is particularly the case when the person being helped is not able to move to a comfortable emotional position at the end of the conversation. When this happens, it is important to remind yourself that the helping process often happens in stages, and these stages need to occur at a pace which is consistent with the internal processes of the person being helped.

If you don't deal with your own feelings of discomfort when someone fails to find a suitable solution, you may well continue the conversation beyond the point where it is useful in order to continue trying to help the person find a solution. If you do this, you will not be helping them, instead you will most likely raise their anxiety and sense of confusion. It is much better to accept that, for the time being, the person is stuck.

> It can be OK to be stuck!

If *you* are able to accept that it is okay for a person to be stuck, then that person may also be accepting of this position. If they can accept that they are not able to find a solution or are not ready to make a decision, then some of the pressure which they have experienced will diminish so that they feel better. Then you will have helped them.

DECIDING TO DO NOTHING CAN BE A VALID DECISION

Sometimes, after looking at all the options, a person will decide that the best solution is to do nothing at all. It is important to remember that this is a valid decision. Often when a decision to do nothing is made, the person's situation will change with time, so that they will end up feeling better. Naturally there is a problem for those people who are in highly stressful and/or anxiety-producing situations, who choose to take no action. However, it is important for you to remember that just by talking about their situation they may feel better, and may be more empowered to cope with their situation. Also, it is possible that later they will make a different decision and will take action to change their situation. We need to remember that people can be helped in stages as explained previously. Today's conversation may be a precursor to change which occurs in the future.

chapter summary

▨ It is better to be person focused rather than solution focused.

▨ We need to respect a person's ability to find their own solutions.

▨ We need to respect a person's right to find solutions which fit for them.

▨ To assist in the exploration of solutions we need to:
  ● Allow the person time.
  ● Use active listening, including reflection.
  ● Encourage the person to explore alternatives.
  ● Use particular questions.

▨ We need to help the person consider the consequences of possible solutions.

▨ Making decisions often involves loss and most people are reluctant to accept loss.

▨ Considering the least desirable option first can be helpful.

▨ Stay in touch with your own feelings.

▨ It can be okay to be stuck for a while.

▨ Deciding to do nothing is a valid decision.

ASSIGNMENT EXERCISES FOR COURSEWORK STUDENTS

1. Find a friend who understands the nature of the assignment and is willing to help you with this exercise. You need someone who has a problem (it could be quite insignificant) which requires them to make a decision. Ask them if they are willing to talk to you about their problem while you tape-record the conversation. It is important that you respect their wishes with regard to the tape recording (and erase the tape if they ask you to do so at the end of the conversation). Use the tape recording to enable you to write down a transcript of the part of the conversation which involves exploring possible solutions. After completing the transcript describe how you think the particular skills you used were useful and make suggestions for ways in which you could have improved the helping process.

2. Think of a situation where you have a problem which requires a decision. Briefly describe the situation. Write down a list of your options and under each option describe the advantages and disadvantages of that option, paying particular attention to any losses involved. Choose your preferred solution. Describe how you felt as you went through the process of identifying your options and their consequences. Comment on anything that you have learnt from this exercise which could be useful when helping someone else explore possible solutions to their problem.

8 Helping people to deal with everyday problems

Throughout this book we have emphasised our belief that one of the most useful ways of helping other people is to listen and communicate with them in ways that will encourage them to talk openly and help them to feel valued. We have emphasised the importance of the relationship between the person offering help and the person being helped. Of particular importance is the helper's ability to look at the situation from the troubled person's point of view.

SEEING THE OTHER PERSON'S PICTURE

We need to let the person who is talking with us know that we have both heard and understood what they are telling us about themselves and their situation. By doing this we validate what they are saying and confirm that we are looking at the situation from their perspective. As they talk to us they will describe their situation in the way they see it. If we try to look through their eyes we will see their picture: the picture they are painting of themselves and their situation.

Understanding the context of the person's picture

If we join with the other person in exploring their picture they will believe that we both understand them and respect their point of view. They will feel valued and are likely to begin feeling better.

In order to be able to understand another person's point of view, and to see their picture as they see it, we need to look at their picture in the context of its wider background. That background will be largely influenced by the person's gender, sexual preference, cultural origins, age and stage in life. Having some understanding of a person's life stage can be extremely useful when helping them. For example, you might have noticed that the way a young person responds to a particular problem is often quite different from the way in which an older person responds. Similarly there may be some issues which may be more predominant in older life stages than in younger life stages.

> It can be helpful to view a person's problems in the context of their current life stage

In Chapter 1 we discussed the example of a mother who might use counselling skills while listening to her teenage daughter talk about the difficulties she has in her relationship with her best friend. The mother's primary role is as a parent, and in that role she might choose to use some counselling skills during the conversation. It might also be appropriate for her to make suggestions and/or give her daughter useful information which she has gleaned from her own time as an adolescent and through her experiences in later life. In particular, because the mother has been an adolescent herself, she is likely to understand adolescent issues and what it is like to be a young person. Having this knowledge about the adolescent life stage will enable her to have some understanding of the wider context into which her daughter's problems fit. Understanding of this context, and remembering what it was like to be an adolescent, will help her to understand the situation from her daughter's point of view so that she is in a better position to be helpful.

It is clear that if we are to be helpful in enabling a person to explore and deal with everyday problems it can be useful for us to understand something of the wider context of their problems. In order to do this we need to:

1. have an understanding of cultural issues
2. recognise the influence that a person's stage in life has on the way they view their problems.

THE INFLUENCE OF CULTURAL ISSUES

Sometimes, when you're trying to help a person by using coun-selling skills, you may recognise that important values and beliefs which they hold are different from yours because they come from a different culture. If we are to give the best possible help to a person, we need to try to understand something of the way in which their culture influences their perceptions, thoughts, beliefs and attitudes. Consequently we think that it might be useful for us to spend some time discussing some important aspects of cultural difference.

The individual in the family

Many people in western society place considerable emphasis on individuality and a high value on a person's individual rights. Additionally, they may believe that the need for a person to fulfil their own potential as an individual should take precedence over the needs of the family as a group. However, within western society there are many people who come from cultural settings which place a much greater emphasis on the family, community, and the need for individuals to have a sense of responsibility for their wider social group.

Cultural differences relating to family values can create particular difficulties for some adolescents. For example in some Asian fami-lies the eldest son is expected to help raise younger children and to be a role model for them. Daughters are expected to help in the household and, generally, fewer demands are placed upon them. Additionally there may be an expectation that they will become members of their husband's family when they marry.

In some cultures children are expected to leave home and become relatively independent from their parents, whereas in other cultures they are expected to retain emotional ties with their mother, and a respectful and deferential attitude towards their father, even when they have become adults.

Can you see how important it is for us to recognise whether the person we are trying to help comes from a culture where individual

143

needs take precedence, or from a culture where the wider needs of their social group take precedence? Unless we recognise and value the cultural beliefs and attitudes of the people we are trying to help, we are unlikely to be able to see the world in the way they see it. Instead of helping them, we may confuse them by challenging values which are important to them.

Even the notion of what constitutes a family varies from culture to culture. In some cultures there is an emphasis on the nuclear family whereas in others the emphasis is on the extended family.

Respect for the young and the old

In some cultures older people, in particular parents and grandparents, are held in especially high esteem. It is expected that respect will be shown to them through obeying them even in adult life. In other cultures children's rights are emphasised as being at least as important, or even more important, than those of older people. In these cultures respect for older people may be believed to be less important. Particularly when we are trying to help someone deal with a family related problem, it is essential for us to try to understand the way they think about their world in this regard. If we don't do that, we won't be able to see the world from their perspective and we will run the risk of saying things which are inappropriate and do not fit for them.

The expression of emotions

The expression of emotions varies from culture to culture. For example in traditional Chinese culture emotional expression is restrained and not openly expressed except by very young children. It is important to understand this when trying to help people who come from a cultural setting where open emotional expression is frowned upon. If we don't do this we may well embarrass the person we are trying to help.

Response to trauma

The way in which individuals respond to traumatic experiences differs depending on their culture. For example children from some cultures may believe that they are responsible for their own misfortune. Other children may understand and accept their misfortune as a consequence of their behaviour or because it has been imposed on them by an outside agency, or because they consider it to be the result of bad luck.

Gender roles

The expected roles of males and females vary markedly depending on the cultural setting. For example in many Asian families the mother is responsible for socialising the children. Thus, if they become rebellious, she may be accused of poor parenting. The Latino culture tends to be hierarchical, with males being seen as dominant. In this culture there are expectations that boys will be independent and girls will be selfless and sacrificing.

Democratic and autocratic attitudes

In some families decisions are made through democratic discussion and negotiation. However, in other families authority and communication flows down from those who are perceived to have higher status. Thus, in some cultures, the eldest male figure, the father, will make major decisions with little input from other family members. It is clear that understanding the way that cultural differences affect beliefs and behaviours within families is important when we are trying to help someone who is troubled. If we don't understand their beliefs and try to see the world from their point of view, we may set them up for failure in their family environment. This is particularly the case when we are trying to help children or adolescents who need to use behaviours which are acceptable in their family environment. If they behave in ways which are not acceptable in their family they are certain to experience negative consequences.

Spiritual beliefs

Understanding and respecting a person's spiritual beliefs is extremely important. We are unlikely to be able to help someone to feel better if we not able to recognise the influence of their spiritual beliefs and attitudes on their thoughts and behaviours. Not only do we need to recognise differences in major religious orientations such as Buddhist, Moslem, Hindu and Christian, but we also need to recognise less formalised but equally influential belief systems which belong to particular cultures, such as the dreamtime spirituality of indigenous Australians. Additionally, New-Age beliefs are becoming more common in western society.

Differences in spiritual beliefs also have wider implications in terms of an individual's understanding of the world in which they live. For example, while many people believe in the efficacy of modern medicine, others are very suspicious of modern medical practice and prefer traditional and/or alternative approaches.

Holding on to our own values

As we mentioned in Chapter 2, when we feel strongly about moral issues, and in particular issues related to gender, respect and power, it is tempting for us to try to persuade other people to accept our values. While it is generally appropriate for us to try to actively promote beliefs and attitudes which we believe will lead to a better world, when we are in the process of helping someone who is troubled we need to try to understand their belief system so that we can see the world the way they do. However, there are situations in which it is imperative for us to be very clear about our position with regard to particular moral values. For example if we are trying to help someone who has been subjected to physical or emotional violence or abuse, regardless of their culture, we need to be clear in stating our belief that abuse is not okay. Thus, in seeing the world from another person's point of view, we need to be honest and open about our differences while respecting the other person's right to hold on to their attitudes and beliefs, if that is what they wish.

> To be genuine we need to the open about our own beliefs
> and values

LIFE STAGES

As we grow up we go through a variety of life stages. We start as
an infant, grow into childhood, and progressively move from
childhood into adolescence, and then into early, middle and older
adulthood. At each stage of development we face specific challenges and need to accomplish particular tasks if we are to move
comfortably and adaptively into the next stage of life. For example
adolescents need to learn the skills required to enable them to join
the workforce so that they can progress satisfactorily into the
young adult stage in life.

As a helper it can be very useful to know how the various stages in
life influence the way that a person perceives their problems and
difficulties. By having this information we are in a better position
to see their picture in the context of the important challenges and
tasks relevant for their particular stage in life. If we can do this we
will be better equipped to help them.

DEALING WITH EVERYDAY PROBLEMS IN
CHILDHOOD

Because a child is dependent on their mother, father and other
adults around them for guidance, emotional and physical support,
it is natural for their family to control how they view the world
around them. The relationships a child has with others will be
based on their family's beliefs, perspectives, rules and values. It
follows that when a child is talking to us we need to remember that
what they are saying is inevitably influenced by the views of their
family, culture and the community in which they live. To be helpful
to a child we need to understand and respect the way they see their
wider environment and their place in it.

> A child's family influences the way they view the world

At a personal level, all children need to feel safe and loved. Children will feel insecure if the world around them is not safe and if there is nobody they can turn to who values them. Understanding that children have this need is helpful when dealing with their emotional behaviour.

It is important for children to feel competent and good about themselves. Experiencing success in school, in sporting activities, or when learning new skills, such as making a cake or playing a musical instrument, contributes to a child feeling good about themself.

> Children need to feel valued and to feel good about themselves

Have you noticed that older children tend to be more aware of themselves and their accomplishments than younger children? Also, have you noticed that children tend to compare themselves with other children and compare their own families with other families?

Friendships are an important part of the childhood phase. Children are inclined to make great sacrifices and compromises for the sake of maintaining particular friendships. As a child gets older they become concerned with rules regarding fairness and justice, the way they are treated, the way they treat others and the consequences of their behaviour.

Spending time in a culture which is different from that of their family can pose problems for children. This is because the way people relate, the way decisions are made, gender and gender roles, the use of language, and the way individuals respond to physical, emotional or traumatic experiences, vary in different cultures. All of these things impact on the way a child thinks and behaves. Consequently they can be confusing for children when they are placed in culturally different situations from those they generally experience.

You might have noticed that when children are having difficulty with life they often show this through their behaviour. Some children are more able than others to use language to talk about what troubles them. This is partly dependent on age. Additionally, the way in which children respond to anxiety or worry varies. Some children become withdrawn and quiet whereas other children may do the opposite and become loud, boisterous or difficult to manage.

Troubled children

From time to time you may come into contact with children who are troubled and you will be able to recognise this by observing acting out or withdrawn behaviour. Sometimes their difficulties may involve the way they feel about themselves, their self-esteem, their feelings of security or insecurity, their relationships with friends or their performance at school. Additionally, childhood difficulties often involve issues related to a child's family and relationships within the family.

When children are distressed it can almost always be helpful if you are able to encourage them to talk with you, even though they may not wish to talk about their problems in detail. We have found that it is particularly important to respect a child's need not to talk rather than to try to pressure them to disclose information. Paradoxically, children are more likely to talk with us openly when they feel free to keep things private if they wish.

The following example is typical of a situation where a teacher helps a child by using counselling skills:

Samantha and her teacher

Samantha is nine years old. Her teacher noticed that she had been standing quietly by herself at school during the morning and lunch breaks watching other children play. Her teacher also noticed that sometimes she would cry when in the classroom. Using the skills previously described in this book the teacher was able to help Samantha tell her that she believed that she had no friends and that nobody wanted to be her friend.

To help Samantha feel better her teacher began by actively listening, reflecting and making use of short responses. She reflected back to Samantha that she was feeling sad about not having friends to play with in the breaks. While actively listening she validated what Samantha was telling her.

Imagine that you were Samantha's teacher. What would you have done? You might have let Samantha know that you understood how important it was for her to have friends in her class that she could talk to and play with.

In a situation such as this it could be tempting to suggest to Samantha that she go and find another child to play with. While this might eventually be one of the options she chooses, in the early stages of the conversation Samantha is more likely to benefit from knowing that you have heard and understood her problem through the use of the active listening skills including short responses and reflection. Telling her to find a friend might present her with an impossible task if this is something that she doesn't know how to do. Moreover, if she did know how to make friends, she would probably have done that already.

It might also be useful to help Samantha feel okay about expressing her emotions. Imagine that you did help her express her emotions with the result that she began crying. How would you respond?

Later, you might use the skills described in Chapters 6 and 7 to help her move towards exploring solutions. While doing this you might use open questions such as 'How do you get along with other children when they are not in a group?' or 'What kind of things do they say or do that make you feel uncomfortable?'.

Can you see that the most useful thing to do would be to use the skills described previously and to be aware of the way that Samantha sees her world as a child?

Self-blame, powerlessness and helplessness

Often when things go wrong children will believe that somehow it is their fault. An important thing to remember about children is that they have very little choice about many of the things that happen to them, although they do have the ability to make choices and decisions with regard to their own behaviour. For example they can choose the way they respond to different social situations. However, many decisions which affect their daily lives, either in a significant or less important way, will be made by their parents. For example their parents may decide that they can't visit a friend when they want, or may decide to move the family home from one town to another. As a consequence children inevitably feel powerless and helpless at times.

Helping children to cope with serious problems where they have become totally disempowered and feel helpless as a result of events that have occurred outside their control can be complex and take time. In cases such as this, the skills of a counsellor who has training and experience in therapeutic work with children are required so that the child can fully recover, feel better and learn adaptive ways of behaving (see our book *Counselling Children: A Practical Introduction*).

DEALING WITH EVERYDAY PROBLEMS IN ADOLESCENCE

Adolescence is the stage in life which marks the transition from childhood to being an adult. During this stage a young person is expected to move from being dependent to becoming independent, self-sufficient and mature. Generally, a young person will move their emphasis from being part of a family group to being part of a peer group. By joining with friends of their own age they experience what it is like to be on an equal footing with others and at the same time to stand alone as an individual in a group setting. By doing this they experience what it is like to be a developing adult. Because they are developing their own individual personalities, young people tend to become protective about their personal space and resent uninvited intrusions by others, particularly their parents. For example, they may become resentful and angry if other members of the family go into their bedrooms. In order to confirm for themselves their growing separateness as an individual, many young people consider moving out of home and some actually do this.

The way an adolescent moves from childhood to becoming an adult varies from culture to culture. For example in some cultures some of the roles played by children, adolescents and adults are similar, whereas in others they are very different. Thus, in some cultures children are expected to perform work-like tasks when quite young for the welfare of the family. As with children, adolescents may be obliged to continue obeying their parents and holding them in high esteem. Where young people who have been brought up in such an environment are exposed to a different social environment which places a high value on individual satisfaction and personal need, they may find the adolescent transition from childhood to adulthood particularly difficult. They may be confronted by conflict between family values, societal pressure and a personal need to establish themselves as individuals. They may be confronted by the question, 'How can I become an individual within my family, an individual in this society and, most importantly, remain truly myself?'.

> A task for the adolescent is to move from being dependent to becoming more independent

Some young people move through the adolescent stage much more quickly than others. Many challenges face the young person during this stage of development. For example a young person must confront and deal with physical changes to their body, intense emotional feelings and sexual feelings. Adolescents develop their own sense of identity. Because they are able to think more abstractly about issues, they begin to develop moral and spiritual values and beliefs which fit for them, and these may be different from those of their family. They will sift through the ideas they have brought from their childhood, throw out beliefs that no longer fit for them and develop their own. When making new decisions the young person will be influenced by their childhood experiences. For example for some young people the impact of growing up in a family where alcohol abuse or violence was present will strongly influence their attitudes and beliefs about their own relationship with, and thoughts about, alcohol and violence.

> Adolescents have a need to develop their own sense of identity

A major problem for many adolescents who live in a cultural environment which is different from that of their family is distress that arises when the rules and values of their family conflict with those of the world around them. As well as finding their own personal identity they also must deal with problems associated with their search for ethnic identity so that they can develop a deeper sense of belonging to a group.

It is during this stage of life that a young person may find the demands of the environment particularly stressful. For example the demands of school or work may be difficult to manage along with changes in relationships. There are many other issues which challenge adolescents. For example they are confronted by sexuality issues, such as sexual preference and the possibility of engaging in sexual activity; they are negotiating financial independence and facing issues related to employment or unemployment. These are just some of the many issues which are likely to influence the way a young person feels and behaves.

Adolescence is a time when it is natural for young people to experiment and try out new behaviour in response to new situations. This almost always involves risky behaviour at some time.

Adolescents need to consider how to deal with the influence and pressure of their peer groups. They need to make decisions with regard to smoking, the use of alcohol and other drugs, sexual behaviour, risk taking involving anti-social behaviour such as involvement in pranks and acts of bravado. Additionally they need to confront decisions with regard to body image and weight control.

> Adolescence is a time of experimentation and risk taking

Because young people are generally striving to develop their independence and distance themselves from the influence of their families, they will sometimes become resentful and suspicious of adults. They will often find themselves in conflict with those in authority because they are attempting to establish their own attitudes, beliefs, principles, values and behaviours.

We can easily be misled into assuming that some young people are confident and capable when they are not. Typically, many adolescents try to appear as though they are in control of difficult situations to illustrate their independence. In reality they may not have discovered the skills needed to do this successfully.

Young people often view adults' offers of help as attempts to influence their emerging beliefs, values and decisions. Consequently, many adolescents are reluctant to talk to adults about the things that trouble them. For this reason we think that it can be useful for young people with an interest in the subject to learn some basic counselling skills so that they can be more effective in helping each other. Having said this, there are some young people who do value the opportunity to talk with an adult about their emerging beliefs. They can gain relief from talking about the things that trouble them and may also benefit if the adult shares information which they have acquired through their own life experience.

It can sometimes be difficult for an adult to validate a young person's point of view. This is particularly the case when the adult has knowledge from their own experiences that may be in direct opposition to the thoughts, beliefs and behaviours of the young person. However, in order to provide the most effective help, we know that we do need to try to see the world in the way the young person sees it so that we can validate their experience and enable them to move forward.

When trying to help adolescents it is important to remember that they are on a journey where it is important for them to start taking responsibility for their own beliefs, attitudes, thoughts and behaviours. We must remember the adolescent's need to establish a personal identity and to take risks. It might be useful for us to think about a particular case. Imagine you're talking to someone called Patrick:

Patrick

Patrick is 15 years old. He tells you that he is considering leaving school to pursue a career as an artist but is uncertain about how his parents will feel about this. Additionally, imagine that in your opinion Patrick has very little artistic ability despite the fact that he enjoys doing artwork immensely. You believe that he has little understanding of business processes, limited contacts with the art world outside his art class at school, but has an enormous amount of optimism and motivation, believing that he will become a famous artist. Additionally, you believe that he is far too young to be leaving school.

How would you respond?

How would you deal with your own beliefs and attitudes with regard to Patrick leaving school at such an early age to pursue a career in which you think he is likely to have little success?

The most important consideration when dealing with Patrick is to recognise that he is in the adolescent stage of development, and that it is natural for him at this stage to take risks in order to try to achieve his primary goal of becoming an individual in his own right. Additionally, if you are to help him, you will need to try to avoid behaving like a parent, because if you do, rather than joining with you, he will want to distance himself from you.

Although it is hard, what you need to do is to try to see the world from Patrick's point of view, and to validate what he is telling you by using active listening skills including short responses and reflection. It is only by joining with him so that he understands that you can see the world in the way he sees it that you will be able to help him think more clearly about his options. Once you have gained his trust by letting him know that you understand the way he sees things, you will be able to help him look at his options by using the skills described in Chapters 6 and 7.

Thus, in inviting Patrick to talk more, you might reflect back to him his excitement and optimism and then use the skills described in Chapters 6 and 7 to help him more clearly identify and describe his plans and their likely outcomes.

In helping Patrick to explore his options it would be important to help him explore the reactions that he might expect to receive from his parents, so that he can become fully aware of the likely consequences of his plans. It may be that as you allow Patrick to explore his own ideas and talk about his options and choices, particularly with regard to telling his parents about his plans, that he will start to see his ideas in a different way.

We have noticed that with adolescents, the best way to help them change their beliefs, attitudes and ideas, is to help them in a process of exploration rather than to directly challenge them. If you are interested in the way in which counsellors work with adolescents you may wish to read our book *Counselling Adolescents – The Proactive Approach*.

Understanding the adolescent stage of development can be of great assistance when using counselling skills to help young people. Establishing a trusting relationship, being non-judgemental, validating the young person's point of view, using the skills of reflection and asking open questions can help the young person to feel valued and respected while at the same time encouraged to explore their own options and choices with regard to their future. Additionally, adolescents respond positively to adults who are honest and sincere and who do not pretend to be someone other than who they really are.

DEALING WITH EVERYDAY PROBLEMS IN YOUNG ADULTS

The problems of young adults in the age range 18 to 30 years are generally somewhat different from those of older people. This is a stage in life where most people are trying to set themselves up for the rest of their lives with a particular career, home, marital partner and family.

We have noticed that the goals of many young adults seem to emphasise social status, wealth, professional success, comfort and influence. However, you might agree with us that the world is changing and that these changes might bring with them uncomfortable consequences for some young adults. In our changing world it seems at times that nothing is reliably safe or predictable. Unfortunately, although it varies from time to time, the employment situation clearly demonstrates this. Some young adults find it hard to obtain the job of their choice, and the challenge of finding a satisfying and relatively secure work environment presents them with a major life-stage issue.

We belong in a society where work is essential for a young adult's self-esteem, self-concept and general well-being. Young adults who are successful in creating for themselves an identity related to their work environment may start to see work as central to their life. This can help them to complete the adolescent shift from being a child who plays, to being an adult who works.

Young adults who choose to undertake further study are often hopeful, but also apprehensive, about the possibility that they will succeed in finding the kind of work they believe they need and deserve. Many students drop out after becoming disillusioned when they realise they may not get the kind of job they want. Similarly many school leavers worry about finding work. Unfortunately, the vicious cycle of no experience/no work can lead to a lifetime of being chronically unemployable. It is not surprising therefore that problems relating to depression, ideas about success and failure, self-worth, and frustration and futility with life affect a significant proportion of young adults.

> Young adults need to find work, establish meaningful and intimate relationships and feel good about themselves

You might be interested to hear about a young adult we know called Alan.

Alan

Alan's situation is not uncommon for young men of his age. He and his partner have been living together for a year. Alan has been working casually as a storeman and has been unsuccessful in finding full-time work. His weekly income depends on how many days in the week he works. Alan is now 25 and he and his partner would like to get married and begin a family. Because of this plan, Alan is now faced with some troubling issues with regard to his and his partner's ability to find a satisfactory and stable income. They would like to have a secure financial income so that they can be assured of a comfortable future for themselves and the children they would like to have. Not only is Alan faced with the reality of finding work that can provide a higher income, but he is also beginning to be troubled by issues with regard to his own success, failure and self-worth. He's even starting to question his ability to accomplish the everyday tasks required of him.

Can you imagine for a moment that you are Alan's boss and that you have noticed that he is starting to become withdrawn and depressed at work? Can you see how an understanding of Alan's life stage might assist you in helping him to explore the issues that are troubling him, and to look for solutions?

New responsibilities

As a young adult a person continues along the path started in adolescence. Generally, they continue to move from being part of the family group they grew up in, to being part of a group of friends, and then may be ready to move into a couple relationship with a view to starting a family. During this period, many young adults face new responsibilities as they start to recognise that they have to stand on their own feet as adults. There is therefore strong pressure on them to be able to demonstrate that they are able to take responsibility for running their own lives. Often the way their parents respond to their success or failure will have considerable impact on the way they measure their self-worth. This is particularly true for young adults who have been reared in certain cultures. In some families the pressure to succeed where parents have failed or have sacrificed their own opportunities for the sake of their children is extremely strong. Consequently some young adults are troubled by mixed feelings. Because of loyalty to their parents they may experience guilt when they fail to meet parental expectations, and at the same time they may strive to find fulfilment in a different way as an individual in their own right. As they follow their own path they may be troubled by believing that they are betraying their parents by not being true to their cultural and religious background.

Creating significant relationships

As discussed previously, because young adults are moving away from the family they grew up in, their primary relationships are usually with friends of their own age. In this group they search for companionship, love, acceptance and intimacy. Initiating intimate relationships and maintaining them is a challenge as many young adults experience rejection several times before they are successful in finding a long-term partner. Once they have found a partner, dealing with the complexities of intimate relationships can be stressful for them.

> The success or failure of close relationships contributes to the way young adults view themselves

It can be helpful if we remember that young adults are primarily faced with the tasks of establishing their role in life, creating and maintaining meaningful intimate relationships, securing their ideas about themselves and valuing that identity. These tasks are often seen by young adults as frustrating but they can also be a source of pleasure and self-esteem. Experiencing the demands and satisfaction of work, and developing close relationships can help a young adult move from being an adolescent to becoming an adult.

Unhelpful responses to stress

Many young adults become overwhelmed at times by the responsibilities and tasks required of them. Consequently, in order to cope, they may resort to abuse of alcohol and other drugs, antisocial behaviour, and/or thoughts of suicide. Although commonly used, these are clearly unhelpful ways of coping with the stresses associated with finding suitable work, establishing meaningful and intimate relationships and feeling good about themselves.

DEALING WITH EVERYDAY PROBLEMS IN EARLY MID-LIFE

In this section we will explore the problems that often confront people from the ages of 30 to 45 years. Many people find this a very satisfying time of life as they enjoy good physical health, a positive sense of self, competence and power in the work situation and satisfying relationships with a partner. However for others this is not the case because this is a time in life when many challenges have to be faced.

It is a time when many people find long-term and/or lifelong partners. They may marry and become parents. They will be confronted by the challenges related to:

● A long-term partnership and/or marriage
● Broken relationships
● Parenthood.

A long-term partnership and/or marriage

Although establishing intimate relationships begins in adolescence and young adulthood, it usually continues into early mid-life with most people making an emotional and physical commitment to another person. This inevitably leads to decisions regarding living together, adopting new roles in relation to each other, and in most cases with regard to marriage and children.

During this period many people experience pressure from their parents who would like them to live up to their expectations. Messages such as, 'You should get married', 'You should have children', and 'You should sacrifice your career to meet the needs of your children', are likely to put pressure on people at this stage in their lives. Such pressure may present difficulties for some heterosexual couples who decide to live together but not marry, and also for those who choose to have children without marrying. Additionally, the expectations of other people may present difficulties for gay couples who come from families or cultural environments where the value of homosexual and lesbian relationships is not understood and respected.

Broken relationships

Unfortunately, for many people in early mid-life, relationship breakdown, separation and divorce may occur where there has been an expectation of the relationship lasting for ever. This will inevitably have significant impact on each partner's self-confidence and self-image, and will additionally have a detrimental effect on their financial resources. Some individuals will face issues with regard to the loss of a loved one as well as the loss of expectations that their relationship would last for ever.

For some cultures, and for some religious groups, divorce and separation are unacceptable, and this may place additional pressure on the person involved. Many people confronted with the breakdown of a couple relationship will find the dilemmas and compromises that face them stressful and troubling. If you find yourself in a position where you offer help to a person in such a situation you may find that your own values and beliefs about relationships and divorce are challenged. We suggest that you might like to take some time to think about the way you would respond if you were to be most helpful to the person concerned.

A significant percentage of people in this age bracket remarry after divorce. Once again, remarriage may present problems for these people. First, they need to deal with the difficulties which a new relationship inevitably presents while dealing with the grief about their past relationship. Second, they need to deal with the responses and expectations of other people so that these do not damage their new relationship or their own self-esteem. Third, they need to deal with their own feelings, so that instead of seeing themselves as a failure they see themselves as successful for having been able to let go of a past unhappy relationship and enter into a new one. For some people there is an additional challenge which arises later as they have to deal with the problems related to living in a blended family where a child or children may not be their own.

Parenthood

While for some people parenting may have begun in the young adult stage of life it continues into middle adulthood. Many parents will encounter difficulties parenting their children through the various developmental stages of their lives. Most people receive very little training with regard to effective ways to parent and consequently may find themselves feeling incompetent when trying to manage their child's behaviour or deal with their child's emotional issues. They may have difficulty in recognising that they need to change their parenting style as their children grow up and move from being younger children into being teenagers.

Special problems arise for those parents who have the task of managing children with disabilities, particularly difficult behaviours, or mental health problems.

When parents have difficulty in managing their children this will inevitably impact on their feelings of competence and self-worth.

DEALING WITH EVERYDAY PROBLEMS IN LATER MID-LIFE

In this section we will explore the problems that arise for many people between the ages of 45 and 60 years. Common issues relate to worries about the future and ageing.

Worries about the future

During this time in life many people begin to re-evaluate their past and raise questions about their future. For many men and women issues with regard to their long-term personal and financial security become particularly important. Career and work opportunities may be re-evaluated.

As children grow up and become more independent, those parents who have spent their lives primarily caring for their children, usually women, are likely to experience a loss of role. This will put pressure on them as they consider their future with a view to making changes.

Ageing

This is a time in life when many people start to recognise that they are ageing. Not only do wrinkles start to appear, but also there may be an increase in health problems, a decline in physical fitness, and the person may recognise that they can no longer manage some of the physical activities they used to enjoy.

The way each person deals with the ageing process will differ. Some people will deny and avoid the inevitable by behaving in ways that remind them of their youth. Some people, possibly in an attempt to stay young, will explore relationships with younger partners and subsequently leave their current long-term relationship. Others will, with dismay, resentfully accept what they see as a painful ageing process. Many others will adjust to the changes in themselves and in their partners by gracefully accepting the situation.

If we are to help people in this stage of life, we should not forget that their thoughts and feelings about ageing are likely to have a major influence on their emotional well-being.

At this time, some people will face the dilemma of whether or not to care for elderly parents. Additionally, they may be confronted with the loss of older relatives through death.

Men in this age group are often troubled by their lack of drive and enthusiasm in the workplace and may fear or actually experience redundancy. For women the onset of the menopause and changes in their appearance generally can raise questions with regard to the way they see and value themselves. Sexual functioning can be a troubling issue for both men and women.

An example

For many individuals in this stage of their life the issues we have described seem to interconnect and impact on them. Simon is a typical example.

Simon

Simon is 53 years old. Because he began his working career later than his peers he has not had a consistent and stable work history. Simon is married and has two children. He has recognised that his current salary will not provide for his children's university education and the eldest will soon be leaving school. He believes that he is capable of working in a position with a higher salary but is unable to find a suitable job. In a recent visit to his doctor Simon discovered that he has high blood pressure and has been advised to quit smoking and drinking. He has been unable to talk to his wife about his concerns because she seems preoccupied with caring for the family while working in a part-time position.

You have noticed that Simon has started to spend a lot of time with a young female colleague at work, and this relationship has developed to the point where he sometimes takes her to a local bar for a drink after work.

If Simon were to talk with us and we were to be helpful to him, we would need to understand how his past experiences and current life stage are influencing the way he is thinking and behaving. If we understand and respect his perceptions we will be able to use the skills described earlier to help him to talk freely about his problems so that he can feel better and move forward into making some decisions for himself.

DEALING WITH EVERYDAY PROBLEMS IN OLDER PEOPLE

We think that you will agree with us when we say that the problems of ageing are becoming more significant in our society as advances in medicine, better nutrition, and healthier lifestyles, result in people living longer.

We have noticed that many older people who enjoy their lives seem to have quite different beliefs and attitudes to those older people who are dissatisfied with their lives. When we think about this we are reminded of the question, 'Which came first, the chicken or the egg?'. It could be argued that it is natural for older people who enjoy comfortable lives to have positive attitudes and beliefs as a consequence of their fortunate situation. Although this will obviously be true for some people, we think that the converse is more generally true; that older people who have positive beliefs and atti-tudes about themselves and their stage in life are more likely to enjoy life because of their beliefs and attitudes. What we find particularly relevant are the individual's attitudes to the ageing process and their personal expectations.

> Positive beliefs and attitudes are likely to lead to positive outcomes for the individual

If we are able to help an older person to fully explore their beliefs and attitudes about ageing, they may discover for themselves that they do not need to be constrained by unhelpful beliefs. The following is a typical unhelpful belief held by some older people.

An unhelpful belief: older people should give up trying!

This belief can have disastrous consequences. Yes, we do need to be realistic as we get older but this does not mean that it is usually sensible to give up trying.

It is very clear that as people get older they find it harder to perform physical activities which they could carry out when they were younger. Additionally, older people commonly experience a decline in their short- and long-term memory, and a reduction in their ability to carry out more than one or two tasks at the same time. Also, their reaction time and the speed with which they can take in new information may slow down.

While there are obvious signs of decline in ability to perform various tasks as people age, there are significant differences among individuals. There are therefore two different issues that need to be addressed when helping older people. First, we need to recognise that many older people are saddened and disappointed as they discover that they can no longer do what they previously did in the same way or with the same speed. If we are to help them deal with their loss we need to give them the opportunity to talk about this loss and to validate what they are telling us. Second, we need to help them to feel good about themselves and about what they can still do. We need to congratulate them when, instead of giving up, they learn new ways in which to cope successfully with their new stage in life.

> We need to validate the older person's sense of loss and congratulate them for discovering new ways of coping

A useful task for many older people is to test their own views and assumptions about getting older against reality. As we have pointed out, the capability of each person varies from individual to individual. Similarly the way each individual adjusts to the changes they experience will be uniquely personal. Consider our elderly aunt, Mandy:

Mandy

Mandy is a very independent lady aged 82 years. She has lived on her own for the last 45 years. Throughout her life she has been a very active person. After retiring as a nursing sister at age 65 she continued to be involved in a number of voluntary activities connected with a Christian Church of which she is a member. Until last year, she took pride in picking up a number of elderly people (all younger than herself) from their homes to drive them to church or community functions in her car.

About a year ago she began to recognise that because her reactions had slowed down, she was no longer driving as safely as previously. As a consequence, she stopped driving and sold her car.

What Mandy did was sensible. She didn't stop trying; she continued to help other people but in a different way. She continued to attend functions, at which she could befriend others, by accepting a lift in a friend's car. She started to travel by bus so that she could visit other people to meet her own and their social needs.

You might like to take a moment to think about the impact of these changes on Mandy. If you had been in a position to listen to her and help her, what would you have done?

When Mandy talked with us we recognised and acknowledged that she was grieving. First, and very importantly, she had sold her old car which she had owned since it was new. Even though the car had deteriorated to a point where its appearance was consistent with its age and its roadworthiness was marginal, it had been a 'friend' to her for many years. Second, she had lost part of her self-image as a person who helped other people by providing them with transport. We helped her to recognise, own and talk about her losses.

We also helped Mandy to recognise her positive attitude. She was able to feel proud of herself for learning to travel by bus after not having used one for many years. Additionally, she realised that she had not given up trying to help other people, but was now helping them in a different way.

Of course, we need to recognise that in the future there may be further losses for Mandy. Whatever they are, we are hopeful that she will not give up trying but will remain adaptable and able to learn new ways of coping with her life stage.

Dementia

For the majority of people, an individual's personality stays much the same throughout life. However, as life expectancy increases, there are an increasing number of older people suffering from dementia.

Serious consideration should therefore be given to older adults who exhibit marked changes in personality as this may be a sign of dementia. Where dementia is suspected, the best way to help is to talk to a qualified professional about the symptoms you have noticed and seek their advice.

Depression and lack of motivation

Depression and lack of motivation tend to go together. People who are depressed tend to have limited motivation. If they are not motivated they are likely to become inactive, and inactivity feeds depression.

Because many older adults experience loss of one kind or another, they are particularly vulnerable to becoming depressed and unmotivated. For example many older adults face the task of adjusting to retirement after a fulfilling and successful working life. They may discover that they are now responsible for caring for an ageing partner who has physical or mental impairment. Also, many older people experience the loss of a lifetime partner and find themselves in a situation where their own physical function has deteriorated to the point where they need to move out of the family home to find more supportive accommodation. The cumulative effects of bereavement and other losses will affect the way an older person is able to adjust to change.

Self-image

In some cultures the extended family is important and the elderly can be assured of a safe and caring environment in which to grow old. In those cultures where the wisdom of older people is valued and respected older people may easily retain a positive self-image. However for others, multiple losses of personal resources and family ties lead to poverty. If we are to help them we need to understand the magnitude of their loss, to help them to talk about it, and to validate their experience. By doing this we may be able to help them feel better and move forward into finding new ways of coping with what is for them a difficult time of life.

Reminiscing

Older people often like to reminisce and enjoy talking about their past experiences. This is generally a useful process for them as it helps them maintain a sense of continuity between past and present. Additionally, it helps the older person to view themselves as someone who has experienced life and made an impact on the world. We can help such people to feel positive about themselves just by using the active listening skills described in this book to give them the opportunity to share their stories with us.

> Reminiscing helps the older person to maintain a sense of continuity between past and present

Towards the end of their lives many older people experience the loss of relatives and friends through death. Consequently, a good listener may provide them with the companionship they need. We can help by lending a genuinely interested ear to listen to them as they reminisce.

Approaching death

Some older people reach the end of their lives alone and without friends or family. As the end of life draws near, many older people need a hand to hold as death approaches. You may find you are the only person available for them. If appropriate, the person you are beside may want to talk to you about their feelings regarding death. In such a situation you may not need to say much, but just to sit quietly and listen. If you feel able to do this you may help them by simply providing them with company and the opportunity to talk to you. However, recognise your limits, and if you are not able to help in this way it may be appropriate to suggest that they talk to a suitably trained counsellor.

UNDERSTANDING THE NATURE OF EVERYDAY PROBLEMS

Now that you have read this chapter we hope that you can see that it can be useful to have some understanding of the nature of everyday problems which many human beings meet in life. You may have noticed that we have consistently suggested that the best way to help people, regardless of the nature of their problems, is to use the skills we have described previously in this book. However, it is also important to recognise your own limitations and to refer to a qualified counsellor if you think that this might be helpful.

chapter summary

▦ We need to see and understand the other person's picture.

▦ It can be helpful to understand the context of the other person's picture in terms of their current life stage.

▦ It is useful to understand the influence of cultural issues.

▦ To be genuine we need to hold on to our own beliefs and values.

▦ A child's family influences the way they view the world.

▦ Adolescents are involved in the long-term process of moving from being dependent to being an autonomous individual.

▦ Young adults often struggle with creating an identity for themselves.

▦ In early mid-life issues of establishing an intimate relationship and/or parenting may arise.

▦ In late mid-life concern is often about the future and issues related to ageing.

▦ Attitudes and beliefs are important in influencing the way an older person copes with their life stage.

▦ Regardless of life stage, counselling skills can be used to help the person feel heard and understood, and to enable them to feel better.

ASSIGNMENT EXERCISES FOR COURSEWORK STUDENTS

1. Imagine that you are working in a nursing home and are talking to an elderly person called Elizabeth. While you are dusting her bedside table, Elizabeth begins to complain of her physical discomfort because she has been sitting in the armchair for too long. Elizabeth tells you that she herself was a nurse in the army during the war and that she recognises big differences in the way nursing is practised today. She seems somewhat troubled about a decision she has to make. She could either return home to her house where she lives with her long-time nursing friend Ann, or move in with her daughter who lives several hours' drive away. You have noticed that, despite several weeks of rehabilitation in the nursing home, Elizabeth continues to need assistance when bathing and toileting.

   Now imagine that you were Elizabeth. How would you like someone to respond to you? What life stage issues would you like them to be aware of so that you felt heard and understood?

. . . .

. . . .

. . . .

. . . .

2. Think for a moment about the way your parents' and family's beliefs, attitudes and values influenced you as a child. Write down two or three
   important ways in which they influenced you.

. . . .

. . . .

. . . .

3. Imagine that you are a classroom teacher who teaches a mixed class of
   boys and girls between the ages of 9 and 10. You have noticed that there
   is a boy in your class who is often unkind to the other children. He bullies
   them in the playground and plays tricks on them in the classroom by
   hiding their pencils and workbooks. You have also noticed that in the
   playground he spends much of his time on his own.

   a. Outline the steps you might use in a conversation with the child using
      Figures 3.1 (see Chapter 3), 5.1 (see Chapter 5) and 6.1 (see Chapter
      6) as your guide.

   b. List the counselling skills you might use.

   c. Comment on some of the issues mentioned in Chapter 2 and
      Chapter 8 when writing your response.

4. In the following scenarios consider how you might respond. In your
   answer explain how your understanding of adolescence might influence
   the way you would give an initial invitation to talk, and help the person
   find solutions.

Scenario A

Amy is 14 years of age and she sometimes babysits your young child. You
notice she is angry and in a bad mood. She has told you that her parents
simply don't understand how important it is for her to spend the
weekend camping with a group of friends. You discover that some of the
young people in this group are 18 years old and that they will be travel-
ling by car to their destination. You also discover that Amy's parents have
not met any of the young people in the group but have heard about

them from their daughter. Amy has indicated that if her parents don't give permission she will find a way of going camping without them knowing.

. . . .

. . . .

. . . .

Scenario B

Daniel is 16. You work at his school in the office and are friends with his family. Daniel's girlfriend has recently broken off their relationship which lasted two years and is now dating someone else at the school. You notice that he is sad, spends most of his time alone, and is untidy and dishevelled and not interested in his usual sporting activities.

. . . .

. . . .

. . . .

5. While out shopping you notice Colin (aged 25) who is one of your son's friends. Your son and Colin grew up together and went to the same school. You begin chatting with Colin. He tells you that he has been repeatedly rejected by employers when applying for a job. Colin believes that he is capable of working in a position where he meets people and which requires good social skills because he believes that he 'gets along well with people'. You notice that Colin seems to be disillusioned, angry and anxious about his future. You discover that he has begun associating with a group of young adults who are unemployed and who receive unemployment benefits. You are aware of this group of young adults and know that the lifestyle they have adopted is inactive and many of them are involved in the use of alcohol and drugs.

    Using Figures 3.1, 5.1 and 6.1 as your guide, outline the way a conversation might go that you think would be helpful in enabling Colin to feel better, and useful in helping him explore his future direction.

6. Sandra is 52 years old and has been married to her husband for 30 years. She tells you that she hasn't loved him for the past 15 years. She is not happy and wants to leave the marriage. She has been dependent upon him all her life and is not sure that she has the courage to leave the relationship She is worried about the future but believes that being in control of her life and beginning a new relationship will make her feel happier.

How do you envisage a conversation with Sandra occurring in a way that would be helpful to her? What issues might arise for you personally with regard to her predicament?

7. Jennifer, aged 50, has been talking to you about her 80-year-old mother who has lived alone since her husband's death three years ago. She describes her mother as frail and being like a child. Jennifer and her daughter Lisa visited Jennifer's mother yesterday. She needed help from Jennifer and Lisa to walk and to cut up her meat at lunchtime. Jennifer tells you that she remembers her mother as being a strong, powerful and ambitious woman when she was younger.

   Jennifer herself is currently studying for her master's degree at university. She is an active sportswoman despite the fact that she has complained to you recently about her aching knee joints.

   What late mid-life issues do you think are helpful for you to know in enabling you to join with and understand Jennifer's picture?

8. List your assumptions and expectations about the ageing process. How might your thoughts and feelings about your own parents or other elderly people that you know influence the way you might talk to an older person?

9. '... the ramblings of old men and women'. What do you understand about this phrase? Describe how you might understand an older adult's current worries through their 'ramblings'.

9 Managing the ongoing relationship

Throughout this book we have been careful to continually draw attention to the need for us to be respectful of the person we are trying to help. This means that we must be particularly sensitive to the person's need for privacy and cautious when inviting them to talk with us so that we are not intrusive. When a person does choose to talk with us openly we have a responsibility to protect and value the information they have given us. Inevitably, when a person shares personal information about themselves with someone else, the quality of the relationship between them will change in some ways.

Sharing personal information can make a person feel very vulnerable. When another person shares sensitive information with us we need to recognise their vulnerability and take whatever steps we can to minimise the possibility that they may feel vulnerable as a consequence of their disclosures to us. There are a number of ways in which we can help the other person to feel comfortable. These include:

1. Finishing the conversation sensitively.
2. Attending to the future relationship.
3. Referring to suitable helping services.

FINISHING THE CONVERSATION SENSITIVELY

We have noticed that many people feel uncomfortable and unsure about how to end a conversation. The way that a conversation finishes will depend to some extent on the setting. For example if a conversation takes place in a work environment there are likely to be constraints on time. Consequently it is important to be clear about your needs and to inquire about the needs of the other person. Sometimes a conversation might need to end at a point where the other person would like to continue talking. In this case it may be useful to invite them to resume the conversation later at a more convenient time.

It can often be helpful to recognise a common process that can be used when finishing helping conversations.

When we are nearing the end of a helping conversation it can be useful to:

- signal the approaching end of the conversation
- summarise
- let the person know that their future actions should not be influenced by our perceived expectations
- give affirmation
- give an invitation for future follow-up
- use a finishing statement
- change the topic, for social conversations.

Signalling the end of a conversation

Often a conversation will end naturally and spontaneously. At other times, the person who is talking to you may want to continue the conversation when you would like to finish it. You may want to finish it because you feel pressured to carry out a particular task or because you know that you have a particular appointment to attend. Alternatively, you may believe that it is sensible to finish the conversation at the point it has reached rather than continue (see Figure 6.1).

Where a conversation doesn't end naturally and spontaneously it can be useful to give an indication that soon you would like to finish talking. By giving the other person some warning that the conversation will shortly end, they will have an opportunity to use the last minute or two to say anything which they think it is important for you to know. The conversation will not end abruptly so the person is likely to feel valued. If you were to end a conversation abruptly, they might believe that you didn't really want to listen in the first place and just wanted to push them away.

> Ending the conversation gently shows that you care

The way you signal the end of a conversation will depend on the setting and the situation. A good way to signal the impending end to a conversation is to make a statement such as, 'I will need to finish talking with you in a few minutes, so I am wondering whether there is anything else important that we need to talk about'.

Unfortunately, it is not always possible to extend a conversation for another few minutes. The person who is talking to you may have picked a very inconvenient time. For example, you might have an important meeting that you need to attend which is about to start. In a case like this it is sensible to be upfront and to tell the other person about your situation. You might say, 'I would like to stay and talk with you for a while but unfortunately I have to prepare for a meeting which I must attend in five minutes, so I'll have to finish talking now'. However, you may decide to give the person an invitation to continue the conversation at another time.

Summarising

Once you have signalled that the conversation will soon end, it is generally best to give the other person the opportunity to raise anything that is really important that they need to tell you. You might say, 'Is there anything else that you would like me to know right now?'. If there are additional matters that they wish to talk about, then you may need to say, 'What you have been talking about seems to me to be important', and then give them an invitation to talk about additional material at another time, if they wish.

The next step is to summarise the most important points covered in the conversation. If the person has decided on a particular solution to their problem, you might like to describe this.

Imagine that you are a workplace Health and Safety Officer and have been talking with the Chief Fire Officer for a particular geographic area. At the end of the conversation with him/her a typical summary might be:

You've discussed with me a number of problems relating to your concern about the difficulties the fire protection officers have in getting to the sites of fires in time to be effective. These have included problems with the emergency phone service, problems with the layout of fire stations, lack of financial resources, and mechanical problems with equipment. You have explained how, understandably, these problems are causing high levels of stress and anxiety in fire protection staff at all levels, including yourself. My impression is that you have made a decision to document these problems in a report to the Director of Emergency Services.

After making this summary, you will need to be clear that the other person doesn't need to live up to your expectations and to give them affirmation.

Being clear that the other person doesn't need to live up to your expectations

It is very important to make clear to the other person that you do not have the expectation that they will necessarily follow through on any decision they may have made. Our reason for saying this is that it is only when a person tries to put a decision into practice that they will know whether it really fits for them or not. Have you noticed yourself that you will sometimes decide to do something, but when you start to do it you feel uncomfortable with what you are doing? When this happens you are likely to change your mind and do something different.

In the example involving the Chief Fire Officer, after giving the summary as described above, you might say:

Although you have decided to write to the Director of Emergency Services you have also pointed out that there might be some disadvantages in doing this. I think that what is important is that you should do what feels right for you, regardless of what that is.

By saying this, you acknowledge the possibility that the Chief Fire Officer may decide to make an alternative decision.

Giving affirmation

When a person chooses to disclose sensitive and/or personal information with us, they take a risk in exposing something of themselves and also demonstrate a high level of trust. Sometimes after talking they may feel embarrassed and question whether or not they will be respected for having talked so openly. Because of this it is important for us to give the person we are trying to help some clear messages of affirmation so that they fully understand that we believe what they have done in disclosing to us has been appropriate, sensible and useful.

> Affirmations must be genuine or they may seem patronising

Depending on the situation and the nature of our relationship with the person concerned, we might make use of statements such as the following in order to help them feel good about what they have done in talking with us:

Thank you for talking with me about these problems. I feel privileged to know that you have trusted me enough to share them with me.

I appreciate what you have done in talking with me this way. In the same way that you have talked with me today, I have found that it has been useful for me to talk with someone else when I have been troubled by things.

Thank you for sharing that information with me. I think that it was sensible for you to talk with me in the way you have.

It must had taken some courage to share this problem with me. Thank you for putting your trust in me.

Giving an invitation for the future

At the end of a conversation you may decide to invite the person who is sharing with you to talk to you again at some time in the future, if they wish. Before giving such an invitation you do need to consider the appropriateness of this. Factors which might affect your decision include:

- the nature of your social or work-related relationship with the person
- the need to set limits
- dependency issues
- the need for referral.

Sometimes you may find that when a person talks with you about their personal issues this may compromise your social or work-related relationship with them. For example if you are in a supervisory position you may be required by your employer to carry out performance appraisals on the people you supervise. If one of these people were to talk to you openly about attitudes and behaviours which could negatively affect their performance appraisal, you might be put in a difficult position. Similarly, in a social context, you may believe that your relationships with other people could be compromised if you were given information of a sensitive and private nature about relationships, behaviours and attitudes of other people in your social circle. In situations such as these, it is both wise and respectful to make clear to the person who wishes to talk with you your dilemma in listening to what they have to say. Once you have made clear the way you feel, you might suggest that they talk with someone else who is less involved with your social scene, such as a suitably qualified counsellor.

> Be ready to refer to a qualified counsellor when necessary

In situations where you have decided that it might be useful for the other person to talk with you at a later time, you might ask them whether they would like to do this by saying something like, 'I am wondering whether it would be useful for you to talk with me again at a later time, or whether you would prefer to leave this conversation at the point we are at now?'. Notice that the invitation gives two alternatives, to continue talking at another time or to leave the discussion at its present point. Giving the two alternatives makes it easier for the person to feel free in either accepting or refusing the invitation to continue talking at another time.

Giving an invitation to talk at a later time may be particularly useful for people who have found it difficult to approach you initially, and in situations where you have been unable to continue a conversation because of some pressure on your time.

Using a finishing statement

Sometimes, after carrying out the previously described steps prior to finishing a conversation, the conversation will finish naturally and spontaneously. If it doesn't, you might decide to use a finishing statement to make it clear that you would like the conversation to end at that point. You might say:

I think it would be useful if we were to stop at this point.

It might be a good idea to stop at this point so that you can think about what we have discussed and give yourself time to make a decision.

I think we should leave it there for the time being.

After doing this, it is very important to avoid falling into the trap of unintentionally inviting the other person to continue talking. Once you have made a finishing statement it is important to realise that if you ask a question or reflect back anything the other person says, then they are likely to continue talking. For example you might say, 'Is it okay for you if we finish now?'. Although that question could have been usefully used earlier, once a finishing statement has been made it may undermine the finishing process, as the other person might say, 'Well I would just like to tell you …' and continue talking. Similarly if you use reflection and were to reflect back what you observed to be the other person's feelings by saying, 'You look satisfied', the other person is likely to tell you why they feel satisfied and the conversation will continue.

Can you see why at the end of a conversation it is not sensible to either ask a question or to use reflection?

Changing the topic

It is common in social situations for people who know each other well to want to discuss their problems with each other. In situations like this the counselling skills described in this book can be very useful in enabling a friend to feel heard and understood, and can sometimes enable them to find solutions to their problems. Often conversations such as these will concern troubling issues, and will involve the sharing of intimate and personal information. Such conversations often happen spontaneously after there has been some general chitchat. In this type of situation, the person with the troubling problem is likely to talk for a while about the problem and then may want to change the subject to talk about something less troubling.

> Changing the topic confirms the social relationship

When using counselling skills to help a friend explore a problem, you yourself may sense that it is time to change the topic of conversation and to talk about something less serious. You might want to check out with your friend, 'Is there anything else you would like to tell me about this problem or would you like to leave our discussion at the point we've reached?'. Then, if they are happy to change the subject, you can revert to more general conversation. By doing this, you are able to normalise your friendship and may be able to engage in some reciprocal sharing of ideas, experiences and information so that the relationship is maintained as a pleasant and enjoyable one.

ATTENDING TO THE FUTURE RELATIONSHIP

When a person has shared some intimate and personal details with you, they may later worry about the impact their sharing has on their relationship with you. It is therefore important to pay special attention to your ongoing relationship with them so that they feel okay about what they have done.

The next time you meet

The next time you meet a person who has shared personal information with you they might be anxious about your future responses to them. One of the things that might worry them is that they may believe that you will expect them to continue talking about the problems they previously discussed with you, and they may not want to talk further.

When meeting again it is important to be positive, open and relaxed in engaging with the other person in a friendly way. Rather than asking them directly about any follow-up to your previous conversation, it is better to ask a general question such as, 'How are you?', or, 'How are things?'. By asking such a question, they can, if they wish, respond by saying, 'Fine'. Alternatively, they can talk to you about how they feel in general, or about how things are in general, without mentioning the previous problem they discussed. An advantage of using such general open questions is that, if the person wishes, they can let you know whatever they have experienced in connection with the problem since they last saw you. Thus, you make it easy for them to feel relaxed with you so that they can resume the relationship they had with you prior to your last discussion, or they can continue that discussion.

Is the person becoming dependent on you?

Once a person has discovered that you are a good listener, they may want to continue talking with you on future occasions. Generally this doesn't present a problem provided that the demands they make on you are not too frequent. Additionally, it is important that you maintain a balanced relationship with them rather than one where you are always in the helping role.

We think that it is important to recognise when a person is becoming overly dependent on you. This is because we believe that all human beings need to learn how to stand independently on their own feet rather than become dependent on someone else. Additionally, it can be very draining for a person to be put in a helper position by someone who becomes dependent on them (see Chapter 10).

Clearly, if you start to recognise that someone is becoming very dependent on you, you need to review the situation and decide on what limits to set. This may be difficult for you because you may have to let the other person know what your limits are. For example a person may have been trying to engage you on a regular basis for fairly lengthy periods of time. If this were to happen, a useful response might be to give the person feedback concerning what you have noticed. You might say, 'I notice that you have been talking to me on fairly regular basis about your problems. I have felt privileged to know that you have been willing to share your personal information with me. However, I am concerned because I don't feel able or qualified to give you the help you may need. I wonder whether you would consider going to see ... (the name of a counsellor).'

We understand that it is often difficult to confront someone who is becoming dependent. However, the very fact that they are becoming dependent suggests that they need help from a qualified counsellor. It is important that when you set limits you recognise that you are not only protecting yourself but are also taking the best possible action in encouraging the other person to seek appropriate help.

REFERRAL TO HELPING SERVICES

When a person talks with you about their personal problems you may discover that they have special needs which require the help of a qualified counsellor or other professional. For example you may recognise that a person has talked to you on a number of occasions about the same problem and that their situation has not changed. You might realise that it is uncomfortable for you to listen to their problem because you are too close to their situation yourself. You might be concerned because you have noticed that the person's thought processes or behaviours are either chaotic, somewhat paranoid or bizarre. In each of these cases it would be irresponsible not to suggest that the person concerned see someone suitably qualified to help them with their problem.

It can be useful to know the names and contact details of helping services in your local area or workplace. If you do this, then you will be able to make sensible suggestions when you need to recommend that someone goes to see a qualified counsellor.

chapter summary

- ■ We need to finish a conversation sensitively. This involves:
  - Signalling the approaching end.
  - Summarising.
  - Giving affirmation.
  - Giving an invitation for a future follow-up.
  - Using a finishing statement.
  - For social conversations, changing the topic.

- ■ The other person does not need to live up to our expectations.

- ■ We need to attend to the future relationship. This involves:
  - Dealing with dependency.
  - Referral to helping services.

ASSIGNMENT EXERCISES FOR COURSEWORK STUDENTS

1. Imagine that your boss at work has just disclosed to you that he was caught by the police while driving under the influence of alcohol and is likely to be charged. He has told you that he is afraid that if the senior management discover what he has done, he will be sacked because the company is keen to preserve its public image. He is considering approaching his immediate manager and disclosing his predicament because he thinks that by owning up before his misdemeanour is discovered, he may be dealt with more leniently. He has made it clear that what he has said to you has been in confidence, and that he is not ready to make a firm decision yet about whether to confide in his immediate manager. You recognise that it is an appropriate point at which to end the conversation.

   a. Explain how you would feel emotionally and what you would be thinking at this point.

   b. Write down what you would say to your boss in order to close the conversation.

   c. Write down what you would say to him the next time you met him.

2. Imagine that your best friend has told you that she became angry and verbally abused her daughter when she discovered that she had been using illegal drugs. Your friend made it clear that she now feels guilty on two counts. First, she believes that she has been a bad role model because her daughter has seen her abusing alcohol in the past. Second, she realises that she may have damaged her relationship with her daughter because of the angry and abusive outburst. She told you that she is very fond of her daughter, realises that she cares about her a great deal and is worried because she wants her daughter to succeed in life. She believes that if her daughter continues to use illegal drugs she will damage her future possibilities.

   a. It is time to close the conversation. What would you say to your friend?

   b. What would you say to her next time you met?

3. In each of the following situations imagine that you have decided that it would be sensible to refer the person who has been talking with you to someone more qualified to help:

   a. The person who has been talking to you has indicated that they have a drug and alcohol problem.

   b. The person who has been talking to you has let you know that they have no money and have run out of food.

   c. You have noticed that the person who has been talking to you has been very depressed for a long time.

   d. You have noticed that the person who has been talking to you has thoughts which seem to you to be bizarre and out of touch with reality.

   e. The person who has been talking to you has confided that they are worried they may be suffering from a sexually transmitted disease but have been afraid to seek medical attention.

   For each of the above situations:

   ● Explain what, if anything, you would do (give your reasons).

   ● Describe what you would say to the person.

   ● Write down the name, address and telephone number of the person or agency you would recommend to the person for further help.

10 Attending to your own needs

While reading this final chapter we suggest that you might like to spend some time thinking about yourself, reflecting on who you are as a person, and thinking about your own needs.

As you have been reading this book you will probably have been focusing on ways to meet other people's needs rather than your own. We wonder, have you had an opportunity to use counselling skills yet? If you have, how did you feel immediately after you used them? If you have already used counselling skills a number of times, how do you feel now? Your answers to these questions are important as they provide you with information about your own comfort levels when using counselling skills, so that you can make a decision about whether to continue using them or not.

If, after using counselling skills, you felt emotionally drained and overwhelmed, then you would be well advised to look after yourself as the first priority and put other people's needs at a lower priority. In fact this is good advice for all of us: if we put our own personal needs first and look after ourselves properly, then we are likely to feel good and be in a better position to be helpful to other people.

> Look after yourself as a first priority

If, after using counselling skills, you felt comfortable, energised and motivated, then you will probably continue to use them at times when you believe they might be useful. If you do continue using them on an ongoing basis it is probable that other people will discover that you are a good listener and will choose to share their problems with you. This might give you a sense of satisfaction in being able to be helpful to other people. However, you will need to continually remind yourself that if you are not careful, you may at times become overwhelmed and exhausted when listening to other people talk about their troubles.

Although helping other people to feel better by listening to their troubles can be satisfying, we need to remember that doing this is likely to have an emotional impact on us. This is because we are giving our time, attention and emotional energy. Additionally we may catch some of the other person's uncomfortable emotional feelings, because emotional feelings can be contagious. Although we may receive satisfaction from knowing that we are helping someone feel better, the process can be draining for us and if we are not careful we may start to feel exhausted and overwhelmed.

If you decide that you want to continue using counselling skills to be helpful to others, then you will need to think about your own needs and how you are going to manage the task of looking after yourself so that you feel okay. We know from our own experience that if we do not take care of our own physical, social and emotional needs, then we are less likely to be able to be of help to other people.

At times each of us will recognise that we are starting to feel stressed and overwhelmed as a consequence of listening to other people's problems. We ourselves have recognised that we start behaving differently when we are beginning to feel stressed and overwhelmed. Is it the same for you?

Clearly it is sensible for all of us to avoid becoming overloaded and exhausted. We can do this if we recognise our individual signs and symptoms indicating that this is starting to happen. Additionally, people who know us well may sometimes help us to recognise that we are starting to become stressed and behaving differently. When we receive such feedback, or recognise our own warning signs, we believe that it is time to recharge our batteries!

RECOGNISING THE NEED TO RECHARGE

No one has an inexhaustible supply of energy. It doesn't matter who we are, what type of work we do, or whether we do, or do not use counselling skills; from time to time we all run out of energy. If we want to feel good and be effective in our daily lives we need to be quick to recognise when we need to recharge so that we do not end up completely exhausted. Three useful ways to recognise the need to recharge are:

- Realising that you are behaving uncharacteristically.
- Recognising your own emotional state.
- Listening to feedback provided by other people.

Realising that you are behaving uncharacteristically

When we are feeling energised we are fully in charge of our lives and in control of the decisions we make. We are alert, motivated and aware of what's happening inside us and around us. In comparison, when we get stressed and become exhausted we may begin to feel as though we are not in control, but are being controlled by the demands made on us by other people.

As discussed previously, helping other people does place additional demands on us. As a result, we might begin to feel overloaded and find ourselves saying something like, 'Everything seems to be getting on top of me', or, 'I just haven't had enough free time lately', or, 'People are making too many demands on me', or, 'People have too many expectations of me'. Additionally we may find that the thought of a few days of peaceful rest away from other people is very appealing.

You might like to take a few moments to think about how you behave when you are beginning to feel stressed or tired and not in control of your life. Do you behave in the same way as you do when you are full of energy or do you behave differently?

We have noticed that when some people are stressed and tired they react by trying to be more in control of their lives. They do this by trying to be in control of other people, by being bossier than usual, overly critical and irritable. If confronted they may deny that they are reacting in this way. Instead they are likely to blame other people. Do you ever respond in this way when you start to feel exhausted or overwhelmed? We have to admit that sometimes we do.

Some people respond differently to stress. They tend to withdraw, be indecisive, lack motivation and become lethargic and disinterested. They might find themselves making excuses and trying to avoid situations that place extra pressure on them. Are you sometimes like this?

> We all have different ways of responding to pressure

As you can see, there are different ways of responding to pressure. Some people are likely to fight to try to regain control when they are starting to feel stressed, overwhelmed or exhausted, whereas others will withdraw. Whatever your response, it is important to recognise the signs that you are becoming exhausted. Once you recognise the signs you can deliberately take action to look after yourself.

Recognising your own emotional state

If you decide to use counselling skills to help other people you must expect, as discussed previously, that people will talk to you about their painful emotions and difficult problems. As they do this you may experience uncomfortable emotions yourself. Sometimes, when you listen to someone else's experiences or situation, you may find that powerful emotions are triggered off within you. For example you may experience a deep sense of sadness, fear, anger or anxiety. These feelings might be related to experiences of your own. Listening to the other person might have triggered off painful emotions related to a similar experience of yours. If your emotions are troubling and persist then you need to recognise them as warning signs so that you can take appropriate action to look after yourself.

Listening to feedback provided by other people

Sometimes when life's pressures are starting to get the better of us we may not recognise that this is the case. We may not notice that

189

we are not behaving in the way we normally do when we are feeling energised. However, when this happens it is quite possible that other people will notice differences in the way we relate to them.

People who know us well, and have good relationships with us, might give us feedback about our behaviour. They might comment directly on our behaviour. For example they might say, 'You're being rather bossy today!', or, 'You don't seem very happy today'. When we get feedback like this it is easy to feel offended and become defensive. Alternatively, we might choose to reflect on what they are telling us and think about what is happening to us internally. We might then recognise that our irritability, bossiness or unhappiness is our response to feeling stressed, overwhelmed or exhausted. If we are able to recognise the signs that we need to start looking after ourselves then we can take steps to recharge.

LOOKING AFTER YOUR OWN WELL-BEING

As we have explained, helping other people can be demanding and it can be easy to overlook your own needs, particularly if you have a busy life.

As we write this chapter we are wondering who you, the reader, are? We, ourselves, are a married couple with a grown-up family. We work together as counsellors and authors and also run training programmes for other counsellors. We enjoy an active social life. We are busy people and we wonder whether you are also. Do you run a business, organise a home, have commitments and responsibilities to children or older family members, or work in a full or part-time job? Are you studying, pursuing a career or retired? Whatever your situation, you have personal needs. If you don't attend to these as a first priority, then you won't feel good yourself, and you won't have the energy required to be able to be helpful to other people.

> If you want to feel good – lead a balanced life

A good way to look after your own needs is to lead a balanced life. You may want to think for a moment and ask yourself, 'How do I balance my life so that I can fulfil my goals, carry out my responsibilities and at the same time enjoy life?'.

A balanced life will generally include the following:

- Physical fitness
- Entertainment
- Rest
- Creating and maintaining your own social network.

Physical fitness

It is well known that exercise and fresh air contribute to a sense of well-being. The chemical changes in the brain as a result of physical activity are our body's natural 'mood enhancers', 'pacifiers' and 'soothers'. Interestingly, they provide us with the energy and ability to think clearly. Simply walking for half an hour each day can be invigorating and help to sustain the energy that a busy life demands. We, ourselves, exercise for about 40 minutes before breakfast each morning. Sometimes we walk and sometimes we ride our bikes. We have to admit that it takes self-discipline to do this regularly, but we have found that on the occasions when we have temporarily stopped exercising daily, we have had less energy available to enable us to do our day's work. Somehow, the early morning exercise helps us to feel good for the rest of the day. Of course we recognise that what suits us may not suit you. You may have a different way of keeping fit.

As well as exercise we know that a healthy diet provides us with the fuel we need to burn to produce the energy required to enable us to enthusiastically and actively carry out each day's work. Skipping meals, or having meals 'on the run', interferes with our ability to adequately nurture, nourish and look after ourselves, so we try to avoid this.

Additionally, although we are sometimes careless in this regard, we try to avoid eating foods that are convenient but are not good for our health or weight! Carrying excessive and unnecessary weight is energy draining. In this regard we are careful not to deny ourselves the occasional treat because we don't like being rigid. We prefer to have a diet which allows for flexibility, moderation and balance.

Entertainment

The old saying, 'All work and no play makes Jack a dull boy', has some truth in it. If we are to lead balanced lives we need to recognise that there is a time to work and a time to play. The way we play will depend on our own personal preferences in seeking forms of entertainment that suit us. By deliberately including entertainment in our lives we can enjoy ourselves, be distracted from the pressures of work and feel reinvigorated.

As we have said, our choice of entertainment will be an individual choice as we all 'play' in different ways. For some a day trip to the beach with family and friends will provide an opportunity to get away from the things that are pressuring. For others getting dressed in clothes we like to go out to dinner or the theatre provides an opportunity for relaxation and enjoyment. Some people find their entertainment through engaging in creative projects such as painting a picture, embroidery or flower arranging. All of these alternatives can achieve the same goal. They provide a diversion from the ongoing pressures of life and are consequently a time of recharging.

When was the last time you 'played'?

What did you do?

You might like to think for a moment about how you like to play. Do you prefer to play alone or with friends? Do you enjoy a particular hobby or have a special interest?

Rest

Because we human beings are all different we all need different amounts of sleep so that we will wake up each morning feeling fresh and alert. Research suggests that for many people between eight and ten hours of sleep is sufficient. Some studies have suggested that two or three 10–15-minute naps can enhance a worker's performance during the day, but most people do not work in situations where this is possible. It is certainly not possible for us!

Sleep deprivation does contribute significantly to irritability, poor reaction time and many behaviours similar to those found in people under the influence of alcohol. Certainly without adequate rest you will find that your energy is depleted and your effectiveness as a helper compromised.

Some people who lead busy and demanding lives find that meditation can be of considerable assistance. Moreover, the cumulative effects of daily meditation are believed to have wide-ranging benefits on thought processes and energy levels.

Creating and maintaining your own social network

Because you are interested in helping other people you will undoubtedly be well aware of the benefits and importance of supportive social relationships. Positive social relationships contribute to a sense of well-being and provide a valuable distraction from life's pressures. Additionally they provide a sense of companionship and belonging.

It does need to be recognised that initiating and maintaining friendships can sometimes be demanding. Relationships do require a level of commitment so that time is given to nurturing them through sharing common experiences, thoughts and ideas. However, good relationships can be supportive, rewarding and energising. They need to have a quality of reciprocity to be enjoyable and provide some opportunities to have fun together.

Take time to nurture your social network whether it be with family or friends. The benefits are well worth the energy that you put in.

TALKING WITH A COUNSELLOR

We have already mentioned that sometimes when you are listening to someone else's problems powerful emotions may be triggered off within you. For you to continue to be an effective helper you will have to face your own emotional responses and deal with any accompanying intrusive thoughts or troubling behaviours. If you are not able to do this spontaneously yourself then the best thing to do is to talk to a counsellor.

Talking with a counsellor can provide an opportunity for you to express your thoughts, ideas and feelings, to self-disclose and gain insight into the reasons for your feelings and behaviours so that you can make sensible decisions and feel better. Additionally, talking with a counsellor might provide an opportunity for you to explore and discover, at your own pace, your strengths and limitations and more about your internal world and the processes you use to produce change in yourself. It is well documented that many people who talk with counsellors experience personal growth.

ATTENDING TO YOUR OWN PERSONAL GROWTH AND DEVELOPMENT

Personal growth and development enable people to live more satisfying and fulfilling lives and to provide a positive model for others. Personal growth usually involves gaining increased self-awareness and insight through a process of being open and willing to explore and reflect on feelings, thoughts and behaviours.

Attending to personal growth and development may include the following:

● Raising self-awareness
● Resolving past and current issues
● Reviewing personal values.

Raising self-awareness

Each time you meet with another person to help them they will meet with you as a person. You bring into the relationship with them your strengths and limitations and your personality that has inevitably been shaped by your life experiences.

If you are to be effective as a helper and to encourage other people to grow and change then you too must be willing to promote growth in your own life. You can do this by seeking to become more fully aware of the ways in which your potential for growth and change has been held back.

It can be useful to ask the question, 'Am I doing in my life what I believe others should do?'.

Resolving past and current issues

To be an effective helper you will inevitably take risks. Simply inviting someone to talk about a troubling issue can be emotionally risky for you. The invitation opens up the possibility that you may have to face powerful emotions within yourself and perhaps be confronted by some of your own troubling thoughts. However, confronting powerful emotions within yourself and resolving past and current issues may be helpful in promoting your own personal growth. As we have explained previously, a good way to deal with such emotions and issues is to talk with a counsellor.

Reviewing personal values

Continually helping others is sure to test your values, beliefs and attitudes. Articulating, elaborating, reviewing and challenging your values and beliefs is likely to help you maintain a healthy and balanced attitude to other people. It can be useful to search within yourself for the reasons you would like to help others and discover what you have to offer the people you aim to help.

PRACTICAL WAYS TO GROW AND DEVELOP

You might like to take a few moments to list ways that would enable you to attend to your own personal growth and development.

We think that some useful ways to grow and develop include:

● Attending a personal growth group

- Attending your own personal counselling sessions with a counsellor
- Sharing your experiences of helping others with a counsellor
- Listening to other people who challenge and confront you with regard to your values and beliefs, so that you can review these
- Attending to your own spiritual or religious belief system
- Exploring opportunities to improve your helping skills
- Meeting regularly with a group of people who share an interest in helping others.

DECIDING WHERE YOU WANT TO FIT AS A HELPER

As we have pointed out several times, many people gain considerable satisfaction through helping others by using counselling skills when it is appropriate and the opportunity arises. For them, the skills described in this book may be useful and sufficient. There are other people who become so interested in the value of using counselling skills that they want to learn more advanced ways of helping people deal with their emotions and find solutions to their problems. Some of these people may be motivated to undertake a course of study and/or practical training so that they can enhance their ability to help others.

Having read this book you might find that you enjoy using the skills we have described and are comfortable with your lifestyle and ability to make use of counselling skills when you wish. Alternatively, you may find that in the future you would like to explore the possibility of developing your helping skills further. You might then ask yourself the question, 'Where do I want to go from here?'.

Figure 10.1 describes a number of different ways of helping. This figure is only a general guide to the possible opportunities available because these will vary depending on where you live.

Can you place yourself on the horizontal line in Figure 10.1 with regard to where you see yourself now as a helper?

If you are a person who would like to learn more advanced counselling skills you might also find Figure 10.1 useful with regard to making decisions about your future direction. In discussing Figure 10.1, we would like to make it clear that we do not believe

Figure 10.1 Different ways of helping

that one particular position on the figure is superior to another. Help can be provided in many different ways. However, additional training and skills are required if you wish to move from the left-hand end of the continuum towards the right-hand end.

Practical help

You will notice that the left-hand position on the line shown in Figure 10.1 relates to the helper providing help in practical ways. For example some ways of helping in this position might be to provide meals for people who are housebound, to shop for elderly people, to take care of children while their parents work, to provide transport for those who find it difficult to travel alone or to befriend people who are alone or isolated.

Practical helpers are generally motivated and guided by their own values, beliefs, attitudes and experiences. Conversations they have with the people they are helping will most likely be reciprocal with a mutual sharing of information. Additionally, the helper might sometimes find it both appropriate and necessary to provide information and/or give direct advice. Many practical helpers have a supportive network of family and friends, although this is not always the case.

Helping by using counselling skills

In this position on Figure 10.1 the helper uses counselling skills, at appropriate times, with the specific intention of helping the other person to talk about their personal problems with the goal of helping them to feel better and possibly make useful decisions.

Many practical helpers also make use of counselling skills. By doing this they not only provide practical help but also have the ability to listen in a helpful way while the person they are helping talks to them about their troubles. For example volunteer workers who are providing material aid to disadvantaged people often find it useful to combine their practical help with the use of counselling skills. As a consequence, they not only address the immediate practical need for material aid, but also enable the person concerned to talk about their situation in a way that is helpful for them.

There are many people who are employed doing work that does not involve providing direct help to others. However, many of these people also find that they can be helpful to their neighbours, friends, colleagues and clients by making use of counselling skills.

When using counselling skills in everyday life it is sometimes appropriate for the helper to provide information and/or give direct advice. It should be remembered that while using counselling skills the relationship will in some respects be different from a normal conversational relationship. While using these skills the helper is primarily a listener while the other person talks about their personal problems. Consequently the person using counselling skills needs to be aware of, and be guided by, counselling ethics and issues (see Chapter 2).

We think that it is useful if helpers recognise that when they use counselling skills they themselves are an active ingredient in the helping process. Their own personality and personal attributes will influence the relationship they build with the person who is talking to them. This relationship is of critical importance to the helping process.

Because of the influence of a helper's own personality and personal qualities on the helping relationship, it is important for helpers to recognise the need for them to attend to their own personal growth and development and to actively seek ways to promote this in themselves.

Although we hope that this book will provide a good introduction to the use of counselling skills in everyday life we believe that the most effective way to learn to use these skills is by engaging in an accredited training course.

Volunteer counselling

Volunteer counselling involves formal training in the use of more complex counselling skills than those described in this book. Volunteer counsellors usually work with a specific client population. For example they may work with street kids, alcoholics or with people who are victims of crime.

Some volunteer counsellors work on the telephone. Telephone counselling can be an advantage for some people because they can talk about their problems and still retain their anonymity. The Samaritans in Britain and Lifeline in Australia are typical of crisis-counselling agencies which use volunteer telephone counsellors. Volunteer counselling often involves rostered shiftwork. This is particularly necessary in crisis-counselling agencies where 24-hour help is available. Thus volunteer counsellors need to be willing and able to commit themselves to working as counsellors at specific times on a regular basis.

It is essential for volunteer counsellors to receive ongoing supervision if they are to maintain ethical standards and a high level of practice. Additionally, volunteer counsellors need to engage in an ongoing process of personal development and growth so that they are in the best possible position to help others.

Counsellor supervision involves debriefing, discussion of casework and learning and/or improving skills. Most importantly, it also involves the resolution of the counsellor's own personal issues which may have been triggered off as a consequence of helping someone else talk through their problems. If a counsellor doesn't resolve their own issues, these will interfere with their ability to help other people with similar problems.

Professional counselling

Professional counsellors earn their living as counsellors and need to be accredited by a specific board or association (dependent on their country of residence).

Professional counsellors require formal education, training and practical supervision. They need to have knowledge in the areas of

199

psychology, human development and the processes of change. They are trained to use advanced counselling skills in the context of at least one well-established therapeutic approach. Commonly used approaches include Rogerian counselling, gestalt therapy, psychodynamic counselling, psychoanalysis, cognitive behavioural therapy, narrative therapy, and brief solution focused therapy.

Some professional counsellors specialise in using one specific therapeutic approach of their choice, whereas others prefer to use an integrative approach that involves using ideas and practice methods from a number of approaches.

Professional counsellors are required to undergo ongoing supervision so that they can debrief, discuss their work, improve their skills and address personal issues that arise as a consequence of their counselling work. They may often find themselves in the position of client in a supervision session as they explore and resolve their own personal issues.

Professional counsellors are expected to maintain their current accreditation by undergoing professional development activities to demonstrate a commitment to ongoing training and development.

Counselling psychologists and psychotherapists

There is considerable overlap between this category and the previous category. However, we have separated this category from the general professional counsellor, because workers in this category have a high level of knowledge, training and understanding of both normal and abnormal psychology. They will have an understanding of human development and the scientific basis for counselling. This would include, but not be limited to, processes of change, social and emotional development, and the assessment of mental health disorders. They are capable of assessing and providing psychotherapeutic treatment not only for people with high levels of emotional disturbance but also for those who suffer from mental health disorders. Thus, they need to have an understanding of the nature of the full range of mental health disorders and to be aware through psychological knowledge and research of the best treatment methods for particular disorders.

Many counselling psychologists and psychotherapists have a commitment to psychological and/or counselling research. As for all counsellors, they practice under codes of ethics. Additionally, they receive regular professional supervision as described for other counsellors.

Some psychologists and psychotherapists specialise in working with a particular client group or disorder. For example they may specialise in working with children, adolescents or families, with people who suffer from disorders such as anxiety disorder, an eating disorder, obsessive–compulsive disorder, or who are suffering from psychosis.

Psychologists have an additional role when compared with other counsellors as they are trained in psychometric assessment processes. Thus, as part of their assessment of clients, they may make use of particular psychological tests or, in professional jargon, psychological assessment instruments. These are tools that enable them to make qualitative or quantitative assessments of their client's emotional or psychological state. For example a psychologist might use specific tests to measure intelligence, anxiety, depression or psychopathology.

UNDERSTANDING WHERE YOU WANT TO BE

Figure 10.1 is useful in describing a range of helping options. Each of these is useful and valuable. We would like to reiterate that we do not believe that one position on the figure is superior to another. Each position just describes a specific way of helping.

Because you have just read this book we assume that you are probably somewhere near to the left-hand end on the line in Figure 10.1. That may be a comfortable position for you and the position that is most appropriate for you in the long term. However, we thought that you might be interested in understanding the range of options available to people who make use of counselling skills in a variety of ways.

If at a later stage in your life you decide that you would like to learn more about counselling you might like to approach the relevant counselling body in your country of residence. For example, in Britain, the British Association for Counselling and Psychotherapy.

We hope that you have found this book useful in describing ways to use counselling skills in everyday life. Additionally we hope that you will get satisfaction from your willingness to listen to other people when they are troubled. We wish you every success in that endeavour.

chapter summary

■ We need to take care of our own physical, social and emotional needs. If we don't, we are less likely to be of help to others.

■ Recognising the need to recharge involves:
  ● Noticing any uncharacteristic behaviour in ourselves.
  ● Listening to feedback from others.
  ● Recognising our own emotional state.

■ To guard against feeling overwhelmed and exhausted we might:
  ● Attend to our physical fitness.
  ● Seek entertainment.
  ● Have adequate rest.
  ● Create and maintain our own social networks.
  ● Talk with a counsellor.

■ If we are to be useful in helping others we need to attend to our own personal growth and development.

Index

Lightning Source UK Ltd.
Milton Keynes UK
UKOW05f1045241016

285994UK00024B/879/P